VOLUME FOUR

The Cycling ANTHOLOGY

VOLUME FOUR

Edited by
Ellis Bacon
&
Lionel Birnie

YELLOW JERSEY PRESS
LONDON

Published by Yellow Jersey Press 2014

4 6 8 10 9 7 5 3

Copyright © Peloton Publishing 2014

Each author has asserted their right under the Copyright, Designs
and Patents Act 1988 to be identified as the author of their work

First published in Great Britain in 2014 by
Yellow Jersey Press
Random House, 20 Vauxhall Bridge Road,
London SW1V 2SA

www.vintage-books.co.uk

Addresses for companies within The Random House Group Limited can be
found at: www.randomhouse.co.uk/offices.htm

The Random House Group Limited Reg. No. 954009

A CIP catalogue record for this book
is available from the British Library

ISBN 9780224092432

Penguin Random House is committed to a sustainable future for
our business, our readers and our planet. This book is made from
Forest Stewardship Council® certified paper.

Printed and bound in Great Britain by Clays Ltd, St Ives plc

THE CYCLING ANTHOLOGY

THE CYCLING ANTHOLOGY

THE NEUTRALISED ZONE

INTRODUCTION BY THE EDITORS

This is the fourth edition of *The Cycling Anthology* and we hope all our readers enjoy the eclectic mix of essays we've compiled this time.

In years to come, 2014 will be looked back upon as the year that Belfast hosted the start of the Giro d'Italia and Yorkshire welcomed the Tour de France and so there is a British core to many of the stories.

Having established *The Cycling Anthology* as a home for brilliant, original writing about the world's greatest sport, we are delighted to have joined forces with Yellow Jersey Press as our new publisher.

As cycling's popularity continues to grow, we look forward to compiling further collections of varied, timeless and illuminating chapters from some of cycling's best writers.

Ellis Bacon and Lionel Birnie

1

William Fotheringham remembers journalist Jock Wadley – a man instrumental in bringing European road-racing to a British audience during a career that stretched from the 1930s to the 1970s, and whose knowledge of the Tour de France was so great that he helped navigate Brian Robinson and the Great Britain team through the 1955 Tour.

THE INIMITABLE JOCK WADLEY

BY WILLIAM FOTHERINGHAM

Sometime in the 1990s, I rode a race in the windy Essex steppes entitled the Jock Wadley Memorial. I didn't make an impression on the race – which was par for the course – and apart from the usual pain and angst it didn't make a huge impression on me. I knew that Wadley had been a journalist, but that was all I knew. There were other memorial events on the calendar for other worthies, and at the time I didn't pause to reflect further.

It was only later that I realised I had read Wadley's words time and time again, years before. As a cycling-obsessed teenager, reading my father's copies of obscure sepia-tinted cycling magazines until my bum went numb, I hadn't been that interested in the names at the end of the articles, only the names within them: Jacques Anquetil, Eddy Merckx, Tom Simpson, Les West, Colin Lewis.

The black and white copies of *Sporting Cyclist* from the late 1950s through the 1960s, between A4 and A5, roughly the size of a quarto hardback book, and the larger format full-colour *International Cycle Sport* from the early 1970s had one other thing in common: they were Jock Wadley's babies. Those magazines clearly mattered to my dad, as they had stayed with us through various house moves before my mother put her foot down and they had been relegated to a box in a cobwebby closet. Since then, they have come to matter to me too.

One passage in bold type stood out, from the very back of the August 1967 edition of *Sporting Cyclist*, penned by Wadley immediately after a cataclysmic event in British sport, and headlined simply July 13. Clearly, the news that Tom Simpson had died on the Ventoux – Wadley's on-the-spot piece and Roy Green's editorial – had had to be shoehorned into the final pages of that month's magazine at the very last moment before it went to press. It was no less a tribute for all that.

'I still cannot believe it, and neither, I am sure, could you until you saw it in cold print, that we shall never see Tom Simpson on a road or track again,' wrote Wadley. 'At the finish, the British team car driver Ken Ryall gave me details of the tragic event which you all know by now.

'In the press room two hours later, there was an unbearable tension when Félix Lévitan came in to give us the dreadful news.

'Dozens of journalists of all nationalities were in tears. Terrible enough that any rider should have lost his life on the road. A matter of the deepest personal distress that the Ventoux victim was not just a champion but a friend of us all.

'This morning at Marseille I saw a photograph of Tom making the last sprint of his life, beaten narrowly by Gerben Karstens in the overnight stage. Tom was laughing heartily and clearly enjoying the gallop.

'I chatted with Tom before the tragic 19th stage started and I knew that he pedalled off towards his appointment with destiny on the Ventoux the happiest of men.'

You didn't have to make a massive mental leap to feel the pain in the words, and imagine their being written at speed by a man in a state of shock. How could that stark black type fail to make an impression as I discovered this new and exotic world? No surprise then that they stayed with me when I wrote my biography of Simpson, *Put Me Back on My Bike*.

* * *

A road race in Essex, some faded back numbers of old cycling magazines, one imposing death notice. That's not all that Jock Wadley left behind him, not by a long way. Twenty years ago, he published *My Nineteenth Tour de France*, his account of following the 1973 race on his bike. The book is a mini-classic in itself for the way it blends cycling history, one Tour, and Wadley's own experiences on two wheels, but the foreword by Wadley's colleague René de Latour intrigues, because of one passage in particular.

'On the Tour de France leader's yellow jersey the initials HD are embroidered, standing for Henri Desgrange, the father of the race. British cyclists would do well to remember other sets of initials such as WJM [Bill Mills] and JBW. Without their written words I believe there would have been no rainbow jersey for Tom Simpson in 1965, no world championships at Leicester in 1970 and certainly no Tour de France at Plymouth in 1974.'

In the same passage Latour also namechecks the late Percy Stallard, the founding father of the British League of Racing Cyclists, or BLRC. Stallard's role in dragging British cycling into the mainstream as the driving force behind the inception of road racing has been widely acknowledged; his running of the Llangollen–Wolverhampton race in 1942 was a turning point in the history of the sport in this country.

Without Stallard, there would have been none of the intense upsurge in interest and participation under the BLRC, and thus no Tour of Britain, no British cycling team in the 1955 Tour de France, no Brian Robinson, Tom Simpson and so on. Putting Mills and Wadley in the same bracket as Stallard and Desgrange, the Tour founder – and this from one of French cycling's senior figures – was quite a claim. How and why could a cycling journalist be so influential?

* * *

Wadley was a cyclist himself, with the same background in the sport as his readers and the British bike racers he wrote about. His roots lay in club runs and time trials with the Colchester Rovers, the club which still organises the Wadley Memorial to this day. It was on one of these club runs that he first heard about the Tour, he recalled in *My Nineteenth Tour*, when the orderly crocodile made an impromptu detour down a muddy lane in the dark, and a senior member compared the excursion to the 'Toer dee France' – the late 1920s being when the Tour, famously, still took its participants over mountain roads ankle-deep in mud.

He found his way into European cycling thanks to an outing to the world track championships at the Parc des Princes in Paris in 1933, and 'returned armed with half a dozen glossy sports magazines packed with spectacular pictures of the Tour de France which had finished a week or two earlier'. That appears to have been that: a couple of years later, having taken himself over to France on more trips he talked himself into an editorial job on the fledgling magazine *The Bicycle*, clearly a more alluring option than working in the family wholesale fruit firm.

The editor of *The Bicycle*, Bill Mills, is another long-forgotten character, the WJM of Latour's piece. Mills rode as a professional in France for a couple of years in the 1930s at a time when this was completely unheard of, and returned home to found the magazine in 1936. The publication acted as a counter-point to the traditionalist *Cycling* – still produced today as *Cycling Weekly* – which was devoted to time trials, track racing and genteel touring articles.

With Mills at the helm and a twenty-two-year-old Wadley in the first flush of youthful enthusiasm, *The Bicycle* went the other way, taking on the mission of introducing a British audience to the exotic world of European professional cycling. Famously, Wadley asked Mills if he should use the term peloton, because the readership wouldn't understand it. 'Yes,' said Mills. 'What *The Bicycle* writes today, the cycling world will be talking tomorrow.' Taking Desgrange as the role model the magazine ran the first 'mass-start' events in Britain, using circuits closed to traffic such as the test track at Brooklands in Surrey and the Isle of Man TT circuit. Those races were the stepping stones that led Stallard to begin organising on the open road in 1942, and thus to the formation of the BLRC.

Wadley moved sideways into advertising with the agency that handled publicity for the Hercules bike company, then in 1951 he returned to *The Bicycle* under a new editor, Peter Bryan. For four years he was their 'man in Europe', following the races on his bike and producing reams of copy. In 1955, when *The Bicycle* was sold to Temple Press, then publishers of *Cycling*, he had no option but to move on. Prompted by Bryan, Mills and a spate of letters from former readers of *The Bicycle*, he founded a new magazine in his own style – *Coureur*, initially an experiment, which was sold mainly in specialist cycle shops. The response was overwhelmingly positive and by 1957 the magazine had a publisher and had become the monthly *Sporting Cyclist*, renamed to avoid confusion with the glossy magazine *Courier*.

Sporting Cyclist was a gloriously eclectic mix, a key factor at a time when allegiance – BLRC or NCU (the National Cyclists' Union) – amounted to rather more than what racing licence you held. This was, after all, a period when cycling in Britain was bitterly divided, when towns tended to have rival clubs, one affiliated to the BLRC, one loyal to the NCU, when BLRC organisers such as Stallard had been banned by the NCU. And as the two organisations fought it out, time trialling under the aegis of the RTTC went off on its own sweet way.

The magazine's initial name, *Coureur*, placed its loyalties firmly with the BLRC. But the content truly crossed all barriers within the sport. It could include local road races in Suffolk or a Bernard Thompson photo essay on the British hill-climb championship rubbing shoulders with a lengthy piece on training with Jacques Anquetil, or a discussion of the hows and whys of a return to national teams for the Tour de France. There were always historical features, many by de Latour, some by the Belgian Charles Ruys.

Wadley was also a fan of long-distance, place-to-place record attempts. 'His heroes included John Arnold, who in 1954 teamed up with Albert Crimes to break the Land's End to John O'Groats tandem tricycle record,' recalls one Wadley protégé, Martin Ayres, adding, 'Jock wrote: "I have seen nearly all the continental Classics, followed the Tour de France from start to finish, almost set up camp in the major six-day races, yet I think Crimes and Arnold gave me just as big a thrill on their lonely epic as some of the highly paid stars of peloton and track".'

The content was a broad church, but there was more. While the Tour de France was placed above other events, being given an edition of its own, the magazine included no value judgements about or distinction between racing as a professional in Europe and riding as an amateur in Great Britain. It was all presented as cycling, all with the same eye.

What catches the eye are Wadley's digressions, for example, on the way the British fit a cotter pin the other way up to the French − cotter pins, happily, are now a forgotten way of fitting steel cranks to the bottom bracket − or the fact that a Belgian journalist wrote Vin Denson as Van Denson and then a sub-editor dropped the G off GB after his name, and overnight he was a 'naturalised' Belgian.

Typical of the Wadley oeuvre was a *Sporting Cyclist* essay from May 1967, a classic example of the 'journalist hits Europe with bike and camera' genre: beginning at Ostend, Wadley headed first for the Tourmalet cafe at Gistel – a purely personal mission, as the cafe had been owned by Sylvère Maes, who he had seen winning the final stage of the Tour de France in 1934, but who had died the year before Wadley's trip to Belgium. 'I had saved the interview for a very important occasion . . . Now I was too late.'

A quick flip to Kuurne–Brussels–Kuurne follows, for a lengthy natter with a quartet of British amateurs racing the support event, one of whom 'entertainingly contributed a kind of conversational gear change, slipping the chain of thought quickly from the facetious to the serious from the Plausible to the Highly Improbable and Downright Impossible'.

He pedals the hundred miles to Luxembourg (where Harold Wilson is spotted getting out of a Daimler) to meet Charly Gaul, who fails to turn up for their appointment, so Wadley makes a rapid visit to the bike shop owned by Nicolas Frantz, Tour winner in 1927 and 1928, to hear tales of how he won the 1928 Tour by riding partly on a Peugeot girl's bike with mudguards and rear light. Finally, he catches up with Paris–Nice just in time to witness the 'fratricidal' battle within the Peugeot team that resulted in Tom Simpson taking the finest – and final – stage race victory of his career.

The whole is told in one lengthy series, held together by the common factor: Wadley and his bike. But Wadley was not just a cycle-tourist who rode his bike and wrote about what he saw. He was a journalist capable of filling virtually an entire monthly magazine with his own output, as he did with *Sporting Cyclist* each September when the edition was devoted to his insights on that year's Tour de France.

The 1964 issue combines analysis of why Tom Simpson failed to match Jacques Anquetil with, most notably, a riveting eyewitness account of the Anquetil–Poulidor battle on the Puy de Dome. 'Poulidor came by, head up gazing at the ever-rising road. Through the sweat and the grime on his face I could read a mixture of hope and disappointment . . . Anquetil's face was white and he looked plainly awful, now out of the saddle now in, moving slowly, oh so slowly . . .' Plus the Wadley touches – 'on the cross-roads a Tour rider was asking a gendarme the way to his hotel. Not *a* Tour rider, *the* Tour rider of the day – Bahamontes. "Congratulations Fede," I called out. "By how much [did you win]?" "Not enough. A minute and a half."'

But it wasn't just about the stars. 'Today, it's hard to imagine how insular the British were back in the

1950s, when Italy, France, even Belgium, were exotic destinations,' says Ayres.

'With this insularity went a certain arrogance born of ignorance. Cycling "experts" who'd never seen a continental race, maintained that British was best – never mind that no Briton had won a world road race title since Dave Marsh took the amateur title on home roads in 1922. Through his writings, Wadley, a devoted Francophile, broke down the barriers. He didn't hector or preach, instead he entertained and inspired cyclists to sample this new world themselves.

'Previously remote stars like Fausto Coppi, Louison Bobet and Jacques Anquetil were profiled in depth for the first time in the UK press [in *Sporting Cyclist*]. The classics were covered in detail, as were the major Tours. All this was presented on glossy paper with striking photos, many of which were shot by Jock himself. Tom Simpson's successes abroad prompted many British riders to try their luck on the continent. *Sporting Cyclist* helped them with practical advice on how to enter races, equipment, local rules and so on.'

* * *

Mills was one of the select group of British industry and media figures who met after the world road race championships in Lugano in 1953 – the Worlds where Fausto Coppi appeared on the podium with his

White Lady – and floated the possibility that a Great
Britain team might compete in the Tour de France.
But it was his protégé Wadley who played an influential role when that actually happened in 1955 after his
old employers, Hercules, had sent a team to compete
on the European professional circuit, and the riders
then went on to form the greater part of the GB outfit
in the Tour.

Sixty years on, it's easy to forget how distant Europe
seemed to anyone in Britain, how alien the mainstream of professional cycling was to British cyclists,
and how green the pioneers such as Brian Robinson
were. Robinson – one of the Hercules men – rode his
first Tour with only half a season's European racing
behind him, and had no one to turn to for advice due
to his lack of language skills, which he developed later
in his career by learning French one sentence per day
from his phrase book.

Hercules' riders had turned up at their training
camp in the south of France not knowing what roads
to ride on, taking maps in their pockets each day in
case they got lost. They had never seen wine before;
not liking the taste when *vin rouge* was plonked down
on the dinner table, they added sugar to it, which
turned it blue.

At the 1955 Tour, there was much for Robinson
and others to learn: how the day's racing might
develop, what the roads were like, what gears to use

for the mountains, how to deal with the mountains, what to eat and drink. Incredible it might seem now, when contact between cyclists and press is limited and mitigated by press officers and agents, Wadley was the only source of information for the riders. Robinson was utterly single-minded in his determination to 'make it' in Europe but crucially had the ability to recognise anyone who might give him advice and to sift the information he was given. The wealth of knowledge that Wadley had gathered – particularly, one imagines, his knowledge of the roads as a cyclist himself – was a critical part of that process.

'Jock was the most knowledgeable guy about,' recalled Robinson, who felt that the *Daily Telegraph* journalist was the only person he could turn to for advice when he rode his first Tour in 1955. The Great Britain team manager Syd Cozens – by no great coincidence Robinson's trade team boss at Hercules – was a track-racing specialist with limited knowledge of France, with whom Robinson had a troubled working relationship. 'Jock was a gentleman, a polite, welcoming character,' said Robinson. The clincher was this, however: 'he could speak French and we knew bugger all'.

Wadley, in an unassuming way, became an unofficial part of the first British team on the Tour. 'He would wander about every night and morning, if there was anything we didn't know about, he'd be sure

to know. We all but lived with him. He had a foot in
both camps. He was just a friend. He knew the roads,
he knew the way things were. If there was stuff we
didn't understand in the race bible, he'd translate it for
us. We depended on him, more so the other riders in
Hercules who weren't as independent as I was.'

Robinson was one of many. Scotland's first Tour
de France finisher, a tough but callow rider from the
borders named Ken Laidlaw, believed he owed his
completing the Tour to the writer. Early in the 1961
race – the only one he rode – the Scot was suffering from gastroenteritis, had been dropped from the
peloton, and was on the point of climbing into the
broom wagon when he was overtaken by a car whose
occupants included Wadley. Laidlaw told the journalist that he was about to quit and was told 'you'll regret
it all your life if you do'. Laidlaw stayed in the race
and a few days later, the Scot came close to winning
one of the toughest stages of the three weeks, at the
Superbagnères ski resort in the Pyrenees.

Vin Denson was among the riders who wrote to
Wadley – 'as do many others', in JB's words – for
information about racing in Europe. His wealth of
knowledge and contacts made him the go-to man at
a time when plenty of British cyclists wanted to con-
quer this *terra incognita*. The advisory role he played
was recognised when he was invited to contribute
to Francis Pélissier's training camps in the south of

France in the late 1950s, by dealing with the letters the Frenchman invited from cyclists in Britain.

One of those who wrote to him for advice, inevitably, was a reed-thin youngster from Nottinghamshire, obsessed with Fausto Coppi. 'Thomas Simpson, (Harworth and District CC), aged 16', wrote asking Wadley to forward some questions to Pélissier, including the concern that he had 'been told that if I race too often I will burn myself out and be no good when I get older. Do you think this is true?' Simpson had ridden mainly time trials at this stage – he meticulously listed his placings, 11th, 8th, 15th, 7th – and cannot resist mentioning that he was the fastest sixteen-year-old over twenty-five miles in the country. The letter was one of Wadley's most treasured souvenirs.

Another to make use of the journalist's European contacts was the Irish pioneer Shay Elliott, who wore the yellow jersey in the 1963 Tour. At the age of nineteen, Elliott had asked Wadley to put his questions to none other than Louison Bobet, the first rider to win the Tour three times; when Elliott was invited to one of Pélissier's training camps, it was Wadley who met him at Victoria station in London and accompanied him to the south of France. In that vein, it was Wadley who suggested to the organisers of the Tour de France, Félix Lévitan and Jacques Goddet, that they invite the great Beryl Burton to ride their time trial Classic, the Grand

Prix des Nations; it is a measure of his stature that they followed his advice.

By the end of the 1970s, not long before he died, Wadley was still acting as a mentor for British cyclists. John Dowling, Great Britain road captain on the Milk Race in the late 1970s, recalls that at opportune moments a dapper little man from the *Daily Telegraph* would quietly manifest himself at the race start or in the team hotel and gently reassure and advise. It was light years away from the image of the muckraking tabloid hack in search of sex and/or drug-related scandal.

As Dowling says: 'In 1977, my first Milk Race, we were the GB "B" team, a mix of young and old riders, we'd come down to breakfast or we'd be at the team bus, and he'd be there with a road atlas with the route marked out on it. He'd talk us through it, he'd probably ridden most of the roads and there would be little tidbits that would help us. He always had something positive to say and he always popped up when he was most needed. He was more than a journalist but less than a team manager. Very much a riders' man.'

As the Tour gradually grew away from its parochial roots through the 1970s, a process of elimination meant the British writer ended up as one of the minority in the race's entourage who had been there in the days when the Tour's caravan resembled a village in which everyone knew everyone else. Martin

Ayres recalls being with Wadley on one of his last Tours. 'Anquetil would just come over and talk, so would Félix Lévitan or Jean Robic or whoever. Even Sean Kelly would speak to him. He opened lots of doors for me. But by 1980 he didn't really like the way the Tour was going – it wasn't as folksy as when he started.' (Complaints that the Tour is no longer as intimate as it was are a journalistic perennial – those of us who were on the race in the early 1990s have similar moans now.)

Wadley was influential in other ways. From *Sporting Cyclist*, two of his protégés, John Wilcockson and Martin Ayres, went on to edit magazines themselves: Wilcockson – whose first article appeared in *Sporting Cyclist* – was the founder of *VeloNews* in the US and *Winning* in the UK, and is still working at *Peloton* magazine. 'Wadley taught me to be a cycling journalist,' wrote Wilcockson in the foreword to the collection of JBW's work published by Mousehold Press in 2002. Ayres was also brought into journalism by Wadley and went on to edit *Cycling Weekly* and *Cyclist Monthly*. One of the fixtures in British cycling publishing, the photographer John Pierce, was brought into journalism through Wadley's links with *Amateur Photographer* magazine, edited by Roy Green, his former protégé at *Sporting Cyclist*.

* * *

If Wadley was able to bridge the divide between Europe and the parochial world of British cycling, that stemmed from several things. To start with, he wrote from the viewpoint of a club cyclist. At many of the events he covered, he was following the action from his bike, as many of his readers did. There is ample appreciation of what stars such as Anquetil and Simpson do, but no sense that they are anything more than 'racing men' – an egalitarian term which seems to crop up a lot in *Sporting Cyclist* – albeit of the highest quality. The sense of distance between 'us' and 'them' was made manageable.

And Wadley never limited his attention to the elite of the sport. 'Jock had an encyclopaedic knowledge of time trialling,' recalls one contemporary, Mike Price. 'Conversation in the car would be punctuated by "we have just passed the start of the Oldbury 12-hour", or "outside that house is a drain where Alf Engers completed the Finchley 25 in record time".' That might not always have pleased his companions in a press car – it's somewhat unfairly taken as a given among most cycling writers that British time trialling is the sport of the damned – but it underlined that Wadley never lost sight of his roots.

What shines through is his joy in the act of riding a bike, in whatever context, be it a two-up time trial with his friend and colleague Jean Bobet or the Paris–Brest–Paris with French *cyclo-touristes*, or his 'tour' around the 1973 Tour. The story of his setting out on his bike from home to buy some eggs from a nearby shop only to stay out for several hours because the road drew him, is one all cyclists can relate to. But in his writing, his pleasure in being in the saddle comes through largely through his use of the first person, something which was eschewed by other writers of the time, such as Geoff Nicholson.

Wadley is always personally involved, be it in a headwind which slows him down en route to his chosen race finish, or a propitious exchange with a cafe proprietor. At times in his reports, he is clearly a fan with a typewriter. 'For an hour or more, the Dubliner was to give me one of the greatest treats of my race-following career,' he writes of a Shay Elliott escape in Ghent–Wevelgem. And like so many fans, Wadley gets involved; offering time checks, drinks and encouragement. That closeness to the action, that sense of being the man on the spot while remaining a cyclist like anyone else, is what drew British club riders to him.

My Nineteenth Tour makes it clear that Wadley was well aware of the paradox that as a journalist you see less of the race than the fans do. He mentions meeting British club cyclists, who envied him . . . 'Do you know the people I envy?' he wrote. 'You. While I have been sitting on my backside in the car you've been climbing the Tourmalet on the bikes. You got here hours before the publicity caravan arrived. You are wearing hats thrown out from the vehicles, you've probably got free samples of soap, cigarettes, Scotch tape and ballpoint pens in [your] saddle bags. You've had a great picnic lunch in the sun . . . Stood here watching the gradual build-up of the atmosphere, the excitement. Advance press cars, helicopters buzzing around overhead, squads of motorcycling gendarmes, the early ones silent, the later ones more businesslike with whistles, then finally all round is the cry "*Les Voilà*" – there they are! I have been on the Tour plenty of times, but I have never yet been *in* it, part of it, like you fellows are.'

'Wadley did not have the literary eloquence of a Geoffrey Nicholson, a writer who could mint phrases that still ring in your memory thirty years on. Wadley's was a more homely style of writing,' wrote Adrian Bell in his introduction to a collection of JBW's work. Bell's contention is that Wadley was an essayist rather than a pure reporter, his accessible, loosely focused style akin to letters home rather than mere reports. Indeed he is at his best when he is at his most discursive, bringing in an obscure pun or (as when interviewing Eugène Christophe) describing his use on his runaround-John bike of an arcane type of back-pedalling brake. Chapter three of *My Nineteenth Tour* is entitled *Arces-Aix at Easter*, a piece of wordplay which only a long-distance cyclist with a knowledge of French would stand a chance of picking up (hint, try saying it out loud).

'Jock had a love of puns, a sharp sense of humour and a keen sense of the ridiculous,' recalls Ayres. 'During a minor event in East Anglia, the race director announced over race radio: "The breakaways are now starting the descent into Bury St Edmunds . . ." Jock relished the incongruity and said something along the lines of "Where does he think we are, on the Tourmalet? I don't believe it's possible to descend into Bury St Edmunds." The incident kept him, and us, entertained for the rest of the stage.'

Wadley's 'wicked sense of humour' (as John Wilcockson calls it) is what his contemporaries seem to remember – Wilcockson describes his 'raucous laugh', his ability when mimicking the stars of the sport. Ayres recalls a very private character, a man who likened close-quarters life in a press car on Tour to his experiences on the Chesil Bank as part of a gun crew in the Second World War. A man who knew his own mind and followed his own road, be it his lifelong refusal to swap Hush Puppies for leather cycling shoes when in the saddle, or his determination to ride the North Road 24-hour. For many of the riders of the time, he was an unobtrusive figure – several don't recall anything about him at all. For a journalist, that could well be something to aim at.

'His essays were not so much a diary as letters

home, and home was the world of the clubman – the keen, specialist cyclist,' writes Bell. 'Events were not reported as if they were simple objective facts, nor were they sensationalised . . . He offered us his thoughts, his emotions and his impressions at the moment of their happening. It was that immediacy, that sense of proximity to the action which the first-person style provides which enriched his description of the terrain, the riders, or conveyed more vividly the drama of the occasion.'

Wadley achieved a feat – nigh-on impossible for most sports journalists – which was to integrate himself into his writing without any sense of navel-gazing, and only rarely sounding remotely sententious or Pooter-ish. If writers tend to avoid the first person, that may be a principle for some of us, but it's also because it is devilishly difficult to get it right. Wadley, on the other hand, makes it look deceptively easy.

* * *

After Wadley's untimely and unexpected death in March 1981, various tributes were paid to him. The first was the organisation of the road race in Essex that bears his name to this day. 'Those first years, so many of us entered to pay tribute to Jock that they were sending entries back,' recalls Dowling. 'Anyone who had ridden internationally had had his help and felt they owed him. The field at the Wadley would be as good as a Star Trophy and the racing was as hard or harder because we raced flat out, as we knew that is what he would have expected.' *Sporting Cyclist* and *International Cycle Sport* are now merely memories, but the Wadley is now one of the longest-established events on the British calendar, after the demise of many of the 'Classic' Star Trophy events such as the Tour of the Peak and Tour of the Cotswolds.

On a baking Bastille Day that summer, Wadley's ashes were scattered on the slopes of the Col du Glandon by a group of close friends after being carried by bike through the mountains. 'I'd met Jock on various Alpine and Pyrenean passes, in Normandy villages, on circuits and tracks,' wrote Neville Chanin. 'He would always spare time to answer my shouts, jump from his press car and chat with us . . . there was always a touch of envy towards us for we were soaking up the race atmosphere from the saddle. It seemed logical and fitting that Jock should attend his final Tour with a party of British clubmen.'

And for a man who had done so much to forge links between his native Britain and the great races of Europe, who had given help to Britain and Ireland's pioneers Robinson, Simpson and Elliott, it was equally logical and fitting that somewhere on one of the Tour's greatest ascents, 'in the rocky Défilé de Maupas where the Torrent des Sept Laux comes crashing down from seven lakes higher up the mountain', there is a little, unknown spot, that is forever part of England.

FURTHER READING

My Nineteenth Tour de France, JB Wadley, JBW
    Publications 1974
Old Roads and New, JB Wadley, JBW Publications,
    1971
From the Pen of JB Wadley, selected by Adrian Bell,
    Mousehold, 2002

William Fotheringham is the cycling correspondent at the *Guardian*. His book *Roule Britannia, Great Britain and the Tour de France*, covers much of the Jock Wadley era. William would like to express thanks to Martin Ayres for his help with this chapter.

2

Anyone for a three-week jaunt around Italy? Sky Sports' **Orla Chennaoui** quickly discovers that covering the Giro d'Italia is anything but straightforward as she pursues overall contender Bradley Wiggins and stage-win-chaser Mark Cavendish from Naples to Brescia during the 2013 Tour of Italy.

Along the way, there's snow, sun, champagne-showers and being shot at to be contended with, in this revealing behind-the-scenes account of life on the road reporting on a grand tour.

LIGHTS, CAMERA, ACTION

BY ORLA CHENNAOUI

How to describe the sound of gunfire? *Bang, bang*? A little bit flat for me. *Pow*? Hmm, a tad cartoonish and somewhat lacking in drama. *Crack*? Well . . .

If I hadn't been in a blind panic I would have had enough time to give this some consideration while sprinting through a moonlit vineyard in southern Italy after stage 3 of the 2013 Giro d'Italia. The circumstances of this incident are a little undignified so I shall try to spare my blushes, as well as yours. Let's just say that covering a Grand Tour from start to finish often involves what you might call, improvisation. We'd already improvised on dinner by stopping at an otherwise empty, plastic-tabled restaurant en route to our hotel where there was a chatting parrot in the corner and a silent mama in the kitchen. Think beaded curtains with a slight whiff of *mafioso*.

Dinner digested, we were onboard our minibus – which was to be our home for the next three weeks – when the call of nature came. The neon-lit signs indicating a welcome refuge for the weary traveller were few and far between, so it was time to improvise once again. We stopped to use nature's bathroom. As the only female on a team of six, when we came to a stop in a darkened part of southern Italian nowhere, I felt inclined to venture further from the road than I may otherwise have done. Alas, in my haste I failed to notice I had taken up temporary residence between a grand old home and what was clearly their vineyard.

And so back to that sound of gunshot. Whether it was *bang*, *pow* or *crack*, when the first rang out overhead I was shocked and just a little paralysed with fear. When the second sounded, it jolted the senses to life and I thought to myself 'Righto, better get going', or blue-tainted words to that effect. When the third, fourth and fifth were ringing in my ear I was already belting it back to the main road, the sound of my own panting matched only by the blast of intermittent gunfire. Whether the vexed landowner was seeking his intruder with the aid of a nightlight and viewfinder, or simply firing warning shots in the air mattered little. There was no chance of calling for help since my mobile phone had dropped from my dress pocket as I sprinted to safety, but by the time I'd made it back to the relative safety of the road, the production manager was already on the phone to the *carabinieri*.

Now I've always loved a good bit of drama, but slamming that minibus door shut and driving off into the night with a screech of tyres and squeal of panic gave me none of the satisfaction I'd have imagined Hannibal and BA Baracus of *The A-Team* enjoyed.

I knew to expect excitement aplenty from my first full grand tour. This, though, was something else.

Benvenuto al Giro d'Italia.

* * *

My early experience of my first full Giro was, on reflection, rather fitting for a race steeped in every Italian cliché imaginable. The passion, the romance, the *tifosi* . . .

In 2013, the British arrived with genuine contenders among their ranks. Bradley Wiggins had stated that the Giro was his main target of the season. Having won the Tour de France in 2012, now he wanted to become the first British rider to win the Giro d'Italia. Mark Cavendish was there for the bunch sprints, initially for the first two weeks, although his success took him all the way to the end. As sporting venues go, Naples, the city that hosted the opening weekend, was as exciting and titillating an arena as could have been imagined. The southern coast of Italy was transformed into a sort of coliseum for cycling.

On 4 May, 207 riders lined up perfectly preened and primed, with Lycra as fresh as their legs. As the collaboration of colour and contours amassed on the start line, the Tyrrhenian waters were glistening in the spring sunshine. It wasn't lost on those searching for an easy script line that Mount Vesuvius provided the backdrop to the initial sprint stage. As riders go, they don't come much more explosive than Cavendish and, once the proverbial touch paper had been lit, the Manx Missile blasted into the leader's pink jersey, the *maglia rosa*, in front of what those beyond the sport might be surprised to learn was a partisan crowd. This Manxman with the Italian soul, not to mention homestead, took his 11th stage win at one of the most evocative races in the world. It was truly a sight to behold.

As is often the case for us though, the hours before these beautiful moments were filled not with awe and poetic reflection, but with something altogether more prosaic. Bloody panic.

Our working day had begun at eight in the morning. Although there were more than six hours to go before the race got underway, we were scripting, scouting locations and starting to film links to tee up the action ahead.

After a few hours sweating it out, while desperately trying to make it look otherwise in glorious HD, we were done. All we had to do was enjoy the race from the air-conditioned comfort of our satellite truck, get in position for the sprint finish, then film the interviews and links for the end of the show. Except . . . except . . . TV is rarely that simple.

For those who are not familiar with the process
of making television, allow me to explain. With any
given programme or series, we try to establish some
kind of theme, a feel of what's to come, if you like.
For the Giro's opening stage we wanted to capture the
magnitude, sense of history and beauty of the race as
a precursor to the impending action. If we were to put
it down on a storyboard it would look like this: cut
from one stunning shot of Naples to another, then
a series of imposing vistas and cultural scene-setters,
all heavy on the drama, building the tension gradually but inexorably, and all backed with big music.
Something to get the blood pumping.

But now, with the stage well underway and half
our work done, the word comes through from the stu-
dio that the original idea doesn't work and that what
they want instead of a slow, steady build-up is action
with a capital A. Instead of seductive slow-mos they
wanted crash zooms straight from the MTV handbook, a gear-change so abrupt it would cause a chain
to come off.

Having to shoehorn several hours of footage into
one hour's programme is no easy task. And, with
the peloton whizzing along the coast back towards
Naples where they would lap the city centre, we
knew that getting to the finish line would be peril-
ous, if not impossible.

Mercifully, this was the Giro d'Italia and not Le

Tour. Whereas the French are fastidious about playing by the rulebook, the Italians have a more, shall we say, Mediterranean approach. With more than 200 riders rapidly approaching the first lap of the circuit, I'm shocked to think we were actually allowed on to the race course with a mere wink and wave of the hand.

So there I was, walking and talking to camera (an industry term, you understand) when I hear the unmistakable whoo, whoo, whoo of the police convoy's leading motorcycle heading straight towards us. Then come the other motorbike outriders. When the first of the camera bikes comes speeding past it doesn't matter whether we've finished filming or not, it was a case of scrabbling together our belongings and getting the hell off that road. In prime position just beyond the finish line, and with multiple live cameras rolling, I have visions of becoming an unwitting news element of the first stage of my first full Giro d'Italia. I'm worried the straps of my handbag might catch the leading rider and haul him off his bike, bringing down the rest of the bunch, so I press myself against the barriers to save the peloton, myself and my dignity.

Sprinting in heels is something of a learned and essential skill for any half-decent female sports reporter (wedges are best, in case anyone needs to know) and myself and the team just about managed to dash to the closest gap in the barrier and squeeze through. What felt like seconds later, the bunch burst

past sending a blowy breeze through the hair and a
blessed sense of relief to the heart. Phew. Job done. Or
at least, career not undone. For now . . .

Britain's winning ways continued the following
day with Team Sky taking the victory in the team time
trial, on the picture postcard island of Ischia. Again
the setting was heartbreakingly beautiful. The sun was
dappling off the crystal clear waters lapping the sands.
The fans were waving flags and letting their team alle-
giances show against azure skies while filling the air
with cheers and the customary banging of barriers.
Team time trialling is considered by many, myself
included, one of the most beautiful of the sport's dis-
ciplines and we couldn't have asked for more.

As such, it's tempting to arrive at the conclusion
that the beauty of any grand tour stage is inversely pro-
portional to the ease with which it is possible to travel
around it. Locations are chosen by race organisers for
their beauty rather than their logistical convenience.
Terrific telegenics trump everything. Every time.
Going by this theory of inverse proportionality, the
ethereal setting of stage 2 would prove that, as with
any paradise, it would be a bugger to leave.

With only one boat servicing the island, the media
quite rightly ranked low in the pecking order. As the
teams and the support vehicles filed on to the ferry,
we contentedly sipped our chilled refreshments on the
beach, and the world didn't seem such a bad place.

But at four in the morning that blissful idyll felt like a world away. After a long wait for our ferry trip and an even longer drive, I had hitched a lift on a golf buggy and was being driven around the Italian equivalent of Butlin's desperately trying to find a 'chalet' that was neither inhabited nor filthy.

We'd arrived two hours earlier to find that check-in was a haphazard affair. Having been allocated a room that was already being happily occupied by a group of rather messy men, and with most of the complex staff either comfortably ensconced in their own rooms or at the campsite bar, it was left to me to chug around the grounds in the dark with the gardener. All I wanted was a place to rest my head for the few hours that remained of the night. We tried room after room and I'll admit I was more than a little grumpy after a couple of hours because by the time we finally found somewhere for me to sleep, there was only two hours of the night left.

Hotels and your experience in them are an integral part of any grand tour. Often, even the stars of the show have to slum it in budget, dormitory-like accommodation as they make their not-so-merry way around the more scenic parts of the country. For us, it's no different. Anything else would be bordering on the sacrilegious. One particular highlight, or perhaps lowlight, of the 2013 Giro was when our first cameraman and our producer, Tom and Tim, had to bunk

down together in a room which had holes in the walls
where there should have been light switches, remnants
of a tatty blind where there should have been curtains,
and a flashing neon light right outside the window
attracting non-existent customers to a completely
empty bar. After enjoying an entirely sleepless night
they were treated to a breakfast of cellophane-cov-
ered croissants and watery coffee by a chirpy waiter
who insisted on addressing them throughout 'service'
respectively as 'Madame' and 'Baldy'. Needless to say
the names have stuck until this very day, much to
their chagrin.

Our real home on the roads of Italy was our minibus, which attracted plenty of envious glances from
the journalists in their cramped hire cars. But looks
can be deceptive. Yes, we had a driver, but we also had
a coffee machine (which didn't work), a fridge (full of
nothing but tinned tuna, don't ask), and a flatscreen
TV (which, you've guessed it, didn't work). But compared to most of the reporters covering the Giro, we
travelled in luxury until the minibus breathed its last
atop Tre Cime di Lavaredo on stage 20, leaving us to
beg a lift down the mountain in the cars and satellite
trucks belonging to Italian broadcaster Rai.

Still, the fun bus had plenty of advantages. With
the blinds pulled down it doubled up as a dressing
room (for me), and a dance floor, for when we missed
our morning coffee and had to jolt ourselves into life

with a daily dose of Daft Punk. It was our little sanctuary, a closed-curtained confessional if we needed to vent about anything that had gone wrong.

In all the big bike races, it feels as if we journalists are competing in parallel to the riders. As they dash to the finish line, we race to meet our deadlines but we never lose sight of the fact that it is only their race that really matters.

Working for a British broadcaster, and one that sponsors a top team, meant that one rider mattered especially: Bradley Wiggins. Team Sky got off to a solid start with victory in the team time trial, which gave their Italian rider Salvatore Puccio the *maglia rosa*. Every rider talks about how special it is when the whole team gets a chance to stand on the podium together and Wiggins visibly delighted in drenching his fellow teammates with champagne.

But the rest of the week did not go quite to plan for the team leader. Some bad luck, punctures, a crash and a bout of the jitters which meant he descended 'like a girl' in the rain (his words, not mine), meant Wiggins finished the first week in 4th place, seventy-six seconds off the lead held by Vincenzo Nibali.

Sir Wiggo is an interesting character and, despite his best efforts, can actually be fairly easy to read. If he's on form physically, he's generally on form personally. Prior to the Giro, at a Team Sky pre-race media day in Wigan, his spirits and form were clearly good.

After the usual race-related questions, I asked him for a bit of banter on his fellow teammates. Last on the list was Rigoberto Urán.

'Rigo? Well he's a Colombian drug smuggler, isn't he.'

Err, come again?

Wiggins laughs. 'Well, that's what he looks like!'

Wiggins knew any mention of the 'D' word in front of Team Sky press officers would bring beads of sweat to their brows. He also knows that when he produces results, he can pretty much get away with anything. Wiggins, charming and cheeky as ever, seemed well on track to produce results.

But once the race got underway, Wiggins kept himself to himself, making it hard for us to gauge his mood. The demands of a daily broadcasting schedule meant we were in the lap of the gods whenever we arrived at the Sky bus. We prayed, begged and hoped that Wiggins would stop and talk to us but that week neither the gods, nor Team Sky, offered us audience with Bradley Wiggins.

In fact, the first time we got to talk to him was on the first rest day, after nine days of racing. People often believe that, as part of the Sky crew, we get privileged access to the team and sometimes that may be the case but in the heat of a grand tour we are treated like just another news outlet.

We were six hours into our rest day transfer from

Florence to Altopiano del Montasio when the call came to say that Wiggins was doing interviews at the team hotel. That was the good news. The bad news was that Wiggins had already spent most of the afternoon facing the media, we were to be the last TV crew, and we were being granted three questions. Like Aladdin and his wishes, we'd have to choose carefully.

Having spent the afternoon watching the clock on the sat-nav countdown to a much-needed rest-day rest, we now faced a ninety-minute diversion and another late night. But when you get the call, the answer is always the same. 'Thanks. We'll be there.' Pedal to the metal, boys.

My print colleagues were already filing their copy in the hotel lobby when we finally ran in, lugging our kit and equipment in the desperate hope that we were in time. I was in my standard travel gear – beach shorts, a T-shirt and flip-flops – and there was no time to change into anything more professional because we were up against it. I've interviewed Wiggins enough times to know that if he's done with the media, he's done. Tide, time and Wiggo wait for no man.

When we made it into the uninspiring conference room that is *de rigueur* on these occasions, Wiggins was sitting in a dark corner, away from the HD-grade lamps set up by the previous TV crew. Clearly he felt the spotlight was an uncomfortable place to be in right now. My original dismay at being allowed only three questions quickly dissipated. I didn't even need a second question to judge how the knight of the road was feeling. He was as polite as he was professional but there was no spark in his eyes. Although only a minute down, and with two weeks still to race, there was plenty to play for. He said all the right things but without conviction. The truth was, Wiggins knew his Giro was almost over. He just wasn't ready to admit it yet. It's never nice to witness a champion throw in the towel but it was no surprise when, four days later and now five minutes and 22 seconds down, he pulled out of the race.

* * *

It was a Giro to forget for Wiggins but for Mark Cavendish it was one he will always remember. The pre-race game plan may not have been shouted from the rooftops but it was to win a stage, perhaps two, and then pull out before the mountainous final week in order to be at his best for the Tour. However, as the race went on, Cavendish found himself in contention for the *maglia rossa*. He knew he could become the first sprinter in five years to win a points competition tilted in favour of the climbers by the Giro's points system.

Before the Giro, questions were being asked about the reliability of the Omega Pharma-Quick Step lead-out train. Having joined the Belgian team from Sky, many expected them to replicate the brilliance of the old HTC train at a few weeks' notice.

Cavendish is widely assumed to have a prickly manner. Now, whether I've been lucky in terms of timing, or whether he saves that prickliness for others, I can't say. What I can say is that I've always found Cavendish a delight to deal with, reliable, engaging and affable to a fault.

Which is just as well, since the pre-Giro press conference in Naples was held in what can be described as a cave at best and a dungeon at worst. Atmospheric for the press, rubbish for those who have to make TV.

With the help of the Omega Pharma press officer Alessandro, Cavendish agreed to sneak away from the waiting throngs and give a few extra minutes to Sky Sports.

Obligatory questions about the race over, I asked him what his favourite memory of the Giro d'Italia was. It took but a beat and a sideways glance before he replied.

'I'll tell you my favourite memory of the Giro,' he said, with a glint in his eye that is familiar to those used to interviewing him. 'My favourite memory is getting dropped with Brad back in 2008. We were there in the *gruppetto* together, and now he thinks he can win the thing!' Then, with a point of the finger: 'Put that in your Sky Sports highlights programme!' And with that he waved a hand and walked off with a spring in his step.

Cavendish gave us plenty to analyse and, indeed, celebrate in the daily show but it's a peculiarity of covering any race as part of a broadcast team that the closer you are to the action the less of the race you get to see. Watching at home from the comfort of one's sofa gives an entirely different perspective to that gained behind the scenes.

As such my memories of Cavendish's five victories are as varied as the action itself. Take stage 6 for example, along the sunny southern coast of Puglia. The route along the 'breadbasket of Italy' was pancake flat and looked like it had been served up especially for him. But while things were relatively straightforward for the riders that day, for us they were anything but.

Having started the day feeling poorly, I lay on the couch in our minibus and dictated my script while Tim, our producer, tapped my fevered ramblings on to an iPad for me to make sense of later.

Having managed to haul myself upright, and having made a considerable effort to make sure I was presentable, I found out that the decision had been made to cancel our programme so I could recuperate.

Instead, the production team back in London would put something together using the 'world feed' – the pictures and interviews filmed by the host broadcaster and usually used to supplement what we were gathering on the ground.

This might not sound like a big deal but there was

no way I wanted to rest. We were just six days into the Giro, Cavendish was racing towards another victory and to be in Italy and not file a report was just not an option, no matter how sickly I felt.

I was grateful that my bosses and colleagues were concerned for my well-being but I stamped the proverbial foot and insisted that we were going to film a programme come what may. If they used it, great, if not, that was their call, but at least I'd know I'd done my job.

Several fevered hours later, we were on track, with the race heading rapidly towards us. We'd just finished feeding our links – the bits of film we'd recorded to top and tail the action – via satellite when the peloton was round the final bend and into the finishing straight.

We dashed to the line just in time to see the sprint unfold and hear the cry over the loudspeaker: 'Eeeeeeet's Cannonball Cavendeeeeeeesh!'

Exhausted but also a little elated, we took up a position in front of the winner's podium as the presentations took place. Cavendish's second stage victory of the race meant he was back in the leader's jersey so we chose to close our package with the obvious 'money shot', Cavendish pulling on the *maglia rossa*. The idea was for me to talk to the camera as Cavendish went through his celebrations behind me. I glanced over my shoulder quickly to make sure our timing was right, and began to speak.

Just as I was finishing, the heavens opened and
Tom the cameraman and I were suddenly drenched.
Curiously, the sun was still shining, there wasn't a
cloud in the sky and there was suddenly the smell of
champagne in the air. Sure enough, another glance
over my shoulder confirmed what I suspected.
Cavendish had spotted us, the only crew filming so
near the podium, and decided to join in the shot.
Cheers, Cav. *Salute*.

I was soaked but we had a great closing image. I
was prepared to take one for the team as long as it
made good telly, even if I had to conduct my subsequent interviews smelling of booze, which gave
credence to the old cliché about the Irish.

Stage 12, from Longarone to Treviso, was memorable for a number of reasons. The weather, so fine
at the start of the race, had already turned nasty but
now it felt as if Mother Nature was punishing us. This
was the day when Wiggins, suffering from a chest
infection, lost three minutes, spelling the end of his
race. It was also the day Cavendish, already Britain's
most prolific professional cyclist in history, claimed
his 100th victory.

For us, it was another cursed day. As usual, we
spent the bus journey from start to finish scripting.
It had been raining all day and our new cameraman,
Simon Gunby, who had arrived to film the second
week of the race, was not a happy bunny. He thought

he was flying out to Italy for ten days of pizza, ice cream and sunshine, now here he was dressed from head to toe in dripping wet plastic.

The combination of sport and bad weather can lead to dramatic pictures but a reporter sheltering under a Sky Sports umbrella is less compelling. The sky was dark, the clouds obscured the stunning vista and the pictures we sent back made the Giro look miserable rather than epic.

The rain clouds seemed to have followed us around Italy. Even in Matera a week earlier, when the weather had been generally fine, the heavens opened seconds before we started filming. If the gods liked bike racing, they didn't show it that day. Within minutes, we were calf-deep in rivers of rain, desperately trying to shelter under the hospitality umbrellas, having left our own in the bus.

A tidal wave of rain-washed banners and road markings passed us and I had visions of us joining them and sliding down the mountain. Word reached us that the organisers were considering moving the finish line back down the mountain to avoid the flash floods at the summit. Good, I thought, by then we'll have been swept down the mountain far enough to see some of the action.

Then, of course, there was the snow. My word, that snow. I should admit that I was allowed to escape the freezing conditions for one stage so I could fly back to

Ireland for a special occasion for my god-daughter. As chance would have it, the day I missed was stage 14 from Cervere to Bardonecchia, on the day the weather was so bad the organisers altered the route to avoid the climb of Sestriere. Then again, everyone else missed it too because the snow and low cloud meant that the television helicopters couldn't fly, the motorbike cameras couldn't get a signal to send their pictures and the race radio didn't work properly. I take my hat off to my esteemed colleagues – Daniel Lloyd and Carlton Kirby of Eurosport, and Simon Brotherton and Rob Hayles of the BBC – who somehow managed to fill hours of airtime with no idea what was happening on the road. *Capello,* indeed.

Not that I was spared the snowy conditions. By the time stage 19 from Ponte di Legno to Martell, the organisers had to take the difficult but admirable decision to cancel the stage. It was the first time in twenty-four years they'd had to do so because of the weather.

By the time the decision was announced that there would be no racing, we were already well on the way to Martell. That day's stage was supposed to cross the Passo di Stelvio, the highest point of the race, where the Cima Coppi prize is awarded in honour of the great Italian climber Fausto Coppi, but the road was completely impassable.

Sky Sports News wanted a live report showing the horrific conditions on the mountain so we had no choice but to go as far up as we could in search of a satellite signal. I've already mentioned that I like to travel in comfort, in beach shorts and flip-flops, which were completely unsuited to the knee-deep snow.

Whether it was the shock of the cold weather, the onset of tiredness from nearly three weeks on the road, or the peculiar delirium that seems to overtake the traveller towards the end of a grand tour, something made me think it would be a good idea to jump out of the bus into the powdery snow in my summer wear for a picture. Laughing at me more than with me, Jamie the cameraman happily obliged.

I should point out that Jamie was our third cameraman of the trip. We were also on to yet another producer, Mark – although these team changes were pre-ordained, we weren't burning people out and sending for replacements. If I'd thought too deeply about the fact that the production staff in London deemed it necessary to send entirely different teams out to Italy to put up with me over three weeks, I'd have got paranoid. I wasn't paranoid, I just thought I was tougher than most. And so, when I posted the picture of me dressed for the beach, knee-deep in snow, on social media it might have, kind of, been seen as me implying I was harder than the professional cyclists who were unable to face the conditions.

An hour later I'd stopped crying and defrosted. Two hours later, Jamie's camera had thawed enough to film again. A whole day later I was again close to tears, frozen to the bone in the blizzards atop Tre Cime di Lavaredo at the end of the penultimate stage.

I was wrapped up in several layers this time when Adam Blythe of the BMC team rode past me on his way to the team bus, with a mocking shout in my direction. Referring to my misplaced bravado the previous day he asked why I wasn't wearing shorts. Coming from someone who had just ridden 210 kilometres in sub-zero temperatures, I suddenly didn't feel so clever. It was time to man up, take the cold, and then cry . . .

While I am willing to concede that shorts and snow don't go, there are occasions when, as a female broadcast journalist, my usual uniform provokes gentle ridicule anyway.

As the race progressed, and despite the withdrawal of Bradley Wiggins, we nevertheless had plenty of reasons to rush to the Team Sky bus after a stage, along with plenty of other journalists. Their Colombian rider, Rigoberto Urán, had climbed into contention for a place on the podium and we would wait patiently outside the bus no matter what the conditions for a reaction from the team.

The team would cordon off an area around the bus and the journalists would jostle for position, with their microphones, Dictaphones, iPhones and old school notebooks poised for the emergence of Sir Dave Brailsford.

Anyone who has ever interviewed, or indeed met Brailsford, can hardly fail to be impressed by the man. He is engaging, polite and always professional, as well as being something of a journalist's dream. Whether talking to him at a training camp in Majorca, or interviewing him with a tear in his eye when the Tour of Britain arrived in Llanberis, which is practically his home town, or asking him tough questions during the 2010 Tour de France when Wiggins clearly didn't have the form, Brailsford lets you into his confidence and will tell you, either on or off the record, exactly what he thinks.

He feels comfortable enough to poke a little fun, sometimes. After stage 10, for example, after Rigo had taken on the climbs with gusto, the knight of the realm greeted me with words that made me feel ever so professional: 'You look like you're dressed for the beach, for Christ's sake – we're in the mountains!' I had actually swapped the shorts for a smart dress, I should point out, but I won't deny that from a sporting point of view it was hardly practical. Again, though, I cite my ability to sprint in heels.

On one of the many wet days I was in my TV presenter's suit when Brailsford emerged from the bus to be greeted by us, a throng of journalists. He took one look at me, then pointed out a female colleague, a print journalist, standing nearby and said: 'That's how you dress for this weather. Look, take note.'

I was immediately envious of my colleague, who I'd not met before, because she was dressed sensibly and for comfort in a knee-length sou'wester, which resembled a two-man tent with a neck-hole, and a pair of what can only be described as wellies with laces. This was, of course, a practical ensemble for 'real life'. Alas, in telly, it would be bordering on sartorial suicide and a sackable offence.

Brailsford can be surprisingly shy so I like to think that by looking ridiculous, I was helping break the journalistic ice. And it wasn't lost on me that the advantage of being the subject of daily, public fun-poking, was that I invariably got to lead the post-race interviews in return, meaning I could get my questions in first.

I am often asked what it's like to be a female reporter in such a male environment. In truth, I have no idea. I have never been a male in this environment so I cannot make a comparison, nor can I presume to know what it's like to be a male in such a male environment any more than I can guess what it's like to be a print journalist as opposed to a broadcaster. All I know is that part of my job involves unpacking my 'wardrobe' from the boot of the bus and doing my hair and make-up in the wing mirror of the satellite truck. I find it simultaneously incredibly unglamorous yet the most fun in the world. Whether I'm treated differently because I'm a woman, I have no idea, but every inter-view is unique to the person conducting it. Anything I offer as a female reporter contrasts with whatever it is I may not offer as a male reporter. Ultimately, I hope the important thing is the sport I cover rather than the sex of the person reporting it.

At the end of the 2013 Giro d'Italia, I was asked by Sky Sports to say which day from the three weeks of racing was the most memorable. I should say that I got in a bit of trouble with Mark Cavendish, as we were en route to a post-race party, for my answer but I'm sorry, Cannonball, my verdict still stand . . .

It's very difficult to have covered British cycling and not be impressed by the performances of Alex Dowsett, the only pro rider with haemophilia, a medical condi-tion you would think is completely incompatible with a sport as hazardous as cycling. I singled out Dowsett's phenomenal victory in the stage 8 time trial, when he started early, set the best time and then sat in the 'hot seat' waiting for everyone else, including Bradley Wiggins, to come home. His sister Lois was by his side and everyone expected his time to be toppled any moment.

But no one managed to beat Dowsett's time and so he won a stage in this, his first grand tour. Witnessing it felt like intruding on a family moment, a triumph for the human condition. In a world of godly Lycra and superhuman efforts, here was something we could relate to on an emotional level. I'll never forget standing in front of the podium as Dowsett closed his eyes and shook his head in disbelief.

I understand why Cavendish berated me for not regarding any of his magnificent wins as my outstanding memory of the race. It wasn't that I didn't appreciate the effort and determination needed to haul himself through the mountains to clinch the red jersey either. Every one of his victories was hard fought and cannot be taken for granted.

But, as a journalist, it is not every day that you witness up close a magical, breakthrough victory like Dowsett's, or watch as they struggle to comprehend the scale of it all themselves. That was indeed truly special.

Over the course of three weeks, having covered more than three thousand kilometres, our little crew had been through it all. We sang karaoke in Florence, had lengthy, heated debates in French about doping, and had numerous pictures taken of ourselves floating above the finish lines of the Giro d'Italia, thanks to the innovative genius of our cameraman Jamie, but ultimately the Giro ended for us as it had begun.

There was a victory for Mark Cavendish and the crack of gunshot. This time, though, the deafening sound came from a cannon firing pink confetti over the central piazza in Brescia to honour the race winner, Vincenzo Nibali, rather than from an irate vineyard owner spotting trespassers using his crops as a bathroom.

As for the final victory, for once we were able to celebrate. Awaiting the *maglia rossa*, the winner of the red jersey, at the Omega Pharma-Quick Step bus after the stage, we were offered beers by Mark Cavendish's teammates as they celebrated his latest triumph. With our broadcasts done the rest, luckily for all, fades into oblivion . . .

Orla Chennaoui is a reporter and presenter for Sky Sports News, who has spent the past few years specialising in cycling. A former news journalist, Orla switched to sport in 2008 when she was appointed Sky's Olympics correspondent. As part of this role she followed Team GB closely on both the road and the track, and made the natural progression to reporting on professional road cycling. As Sky Sports' portfolio in the sport has broadened, so has Orla's role. When the channel won the rights to broadcast the highlights of the Giro d'Italia, thus covering a Grand Tour for the first time, Orla was chosen to anchor the nightly programme. She continues to present Sky's coverage of the Giro, reports annually on the Tour de France, as well as further flung races such as the Tour Down Under, and spends much of the winter at training camps around Europe.

3

The sprint finishes appear to be the most black and white aspect of professional cycling. There's a ferocious battle for control of the peloton, a searing pace and a hell-for-leather sprint. One rider wins and everybody else loses.

Lionel Birnie wanted to explore a discipline that appears to be taken for granted.

Mark Cavendish explains the intricacy of the lead-out process, the split-second decisions that can be the difference between victory and defeat and the pressure of sprinting against the fastest men in the world.

ZEN AND THE ART OF GRAND TOUR SPRINTING

BY LIONEL BIRNIE

Phweeeeeeep.

A long, shrill whistle pierces the air to warn that the riders are coming. Suddenly everyone standing behind the finishing line is alert. The team *soigneurs,* who had been chatting, sharing gossip and enjoying a brief lull in their busy day, are ready to hand out cold cans of Coke, Fanta and Sprite to their riders. The photographers bump elbows and jostle for position behind the line drawn diagonally across the road a safe distance from the finish. They all want the best shot of the winning moment. The journalists and television cameramen are poised to get to work and will soon be rushing after the main protagonists of the day to get an instant reaction.

The whistle sounds again. A motorcycle *gendarme* speeds past and the man from ASO, the company that organises the Tour de France, looks even more agitated than before and gestures to everyone to get back. The riders are coming.

The commentary from Daniel Mangeas, for much

of the afternoon a steady stream of consciousness, is suddenly sharper. The rhythm of his speech during a hectic sprint finish is similar to a horseracing commentator and I can feel my heart rate rise parallel to the intensity of his words.

I'm in Narbonne during the middle week of the 2008 Tour de France. It's a scorching hot day on the Mediterranean coast. The sun beats down so fiercely on the top of my head it almost causes my knees to buckle.

All of a sudden, the riders are in sight, powering towards us. They are a jumble of colours, almost too much to take in during the short time it all plays out. How Mangeas manages to keep his commentary intelligible is beyond me.

And then it happens. The moment when a little figure in a blue jersey stops pedalling and puts his arms up in the air.

'*Cavendeeesh. Mark Cavendeeesh. Troisième victoire du Tour de France.*'

And then it strikes me that these two or three seconds as Cavendish freewheels across the line – admittedly at more than forty miles an hour – is a brief moment of calm, perhaps the most serene moment of his day. The race is won, his rivals have been beaten, and the time it takes to roll to a stop is his.

Cavendish slams on the brakes and lets out a yell. His Columbia team *soigneur*, wearing a sleeveless version of their blue jersey, runs alongside him and is there when he finally stops. They hug. And before Cavendish can even unclip a foot from his pedal the crowd is closing around him. A television cameraman pushes his way to the front, his reporter beside him, the microphone attached to the camera like an umbilical cord.

One of Cavendish's teammates pushes his way through the scrum, then another, and they hug. Cavendish's delight is obvious, his Scouse-lite accent somewhat incongruous. Remember, in 2008 he was still the new kid on the block.

'*We did it. We did it again.*'

This is Cavendish's third victory of his second Tour de France. He's won at Châteauroux, at Toulouse and he will win again at Nîmes tomorrow before pulling out of the race to go to the Olympics in Beijing, but that is not part of this story.

Cavendish pushes his way through the crowd because he has to get a fresh jersey and go to the podium for the prize presentation, then he has to do a round of interviews, half a dozen television stations first, then the radio stations, then he must head to a large trailer and answer questions from the print media, which are relayed to him by a video link. When all that's done, he has to go to the anti-doping control and wee in their jar. Then he can head to the hotel.

Behind him in the finishing straight, the bottleneck caused by all this brings the other 180 or so riders to a halt after they cross the line. They scoot their bikes forwards slowly. Some seem patient enough, others are irritated by the hold up and particularly by the number of people who are in the finishing straight. I can see their point. Two minutes ago, they were racing full pelt down the finishing straight and now they're crammed together like commuters trying to squeeze on to a crowded train. The air, already hot and dense, is incredibly stifling.

I stand still so I don't bash into anyone and just watch them. On the start line in Lavelanet they all looked immaculate. You could smell the washing powder from 180 sets of freshly laundered cycling kit in the air. Now they are covered in sweat and grime, some have white salt marks round their mouths that indicate dehydration, one or two have scuff marks or cuts on their jersey or shorts, the sign they've been involved in a crash. It's easy to take for granted the journey they've been on while I've driven from the start to finish in an air-conditioned car and had time for a spot of lunch and a bit of work in the press room before they galloped into town. Sometimes I have to remind myself that they are the same men.

Later that evening, I am at Mark Cavendish's hotel for the night, a basic two-star place on an industrial estate – most likely chosen because of the size of the car park to accommodate the team bus, all their cars, and give the mechanics space to work. It's not the sort of place you'd choose if you were going on holiday.

I'm there to interview Cavendish for a newspaper. He's still relatively unknown to the British public but, having become the first British rider to win three stages in the same Tour, that is starting to change. My job is to tell people a little bit about who Mark Cavendish is.

I'd read a couple of pieces by a journalist from the Isle of Man that mentioned that Cavendish had been a ballroom dancer as a teenager. This was not widely known at the time and I was interested to know more. I wondered how the lightness and dexterity of the quickstep and the foxtrot dovetailed with the raw alpha maleness of being a bunch sprinter. The two activities seemed incompatible.

'I didn't care if people laughed at me because I was good at it,' he said. 'I could go to a competition and we could be in the top three or win it and that's what appealed to me. That and getting better at something.'

I asked about his earliest memories of cycling and he talked about entering a race on the Isle of Man and being the only one who had a BMX. The others had mountain bikes. He finished last, went home and asked for a mountain bike for his birthday. The first race he did on it, he won.

The next time I sat down to speak to Cavendish

at length was at the track World Championships
in Pruszków, Poland, in spring 2009. A couple of
weeks earlier, he'd won the Milan–San Remo classic
with perhaps the most powerful, desperate, driven
lunge from the line to pip the Australian Heinrich
Haussler by a heartbreakingly narrow margin. During
our conversation, Cavendish talked me through the
last thirty kilometres in almost forensic detail. Every
move he made, every significant move his rivals made,
added up to contribute to that result. Millions of tiny,
unconscious decisions that changed the course of the
race, eliminating the millions of possible permutations
until only one – a Cavendish victory – remained.

Over the years that followed, Cavendish has won
sprint after sprint after sprint. His team, first High
Road, then Columbia, then HTC-Columbia, rede-
fined sprinting in the grand tours, adopting a level of
tactical organisation that has made it almost (but not
quite) impossible to win without the help of a line of
dedicated teammates.

As he ticked off ten Tour de France stage wins,
then twenty and edged up towards Eddy Merckx's
record of thirty-four – which, it must be pointed out,
came in all terrains, flat stages, time trials, hilly stages
and the mountains – Cavendish's skill has almost been
taken for granted. He had become a winning machine
so reliable that the only story worth telling was when
he got beaten.

Perhaps because of that dominance, the nuance of his art has been overlooked. On television it appears devastatingly simple. Cavendish's team line up with ten kilometres to go, they pace him to the line, he sits in their slipstream until the perfect moment to start his sprint and he wins. Maybe that is why his frustration sometimes boils over after a stage, even when he's won, and he becomes tetchy and irritable.

But I think there's more to it than that. There has to be, because it's not as easy as all that. The pressure that comes with being almost totally dominant has to take its toll. And besides, Cavendish is too intelligent, too interesting and too individual to be seen as a robotic winning machine.

I wanted to find out more about sprinting, the physicality of it, the psychology of it and particularly Cavendish's state of mind before, during and after a sprint finish at one of the grand tours, because these men – whether we're talking about Freddy Maertens, Mario Cipollini, Mark Cavendish or Marcel Kittel – are the fastest road cyclists in the world. They take incredible risks and they are defined by only one thing: whether they win or not.

* * *

Sprinting is a pretty simple concept to get your head around. The finish line is painted across the road and the first one over it is the winner. As cycling goes, it's the purest test of speed but it's only relatively recently that organised team tactics have been employed to engineer success.

The evolution of the sprint train can be traced back as far as 1962, when the Belgian Flandria team would pilot their leader, Rik Van Looy, towards the finish. Van Looy wasn't the first to use his teammates to help control the bunch in the closing stages of a race but Flandria were pioneers in making such a concerted effort. Their racing style earned Flandria a nickname: the Red Guard. Being chased down by the Red Guard meant almost inevitable capture.

Flandria didn't assemble a lead-out train as we would recognise one today, instead they massed at the front keeping the pace high enough to discourage attacks rather than prohibit them. Then, when rivals attempted to break clear, the Flandria riders would take turns to jump across the gap and close down the escapes, allowing Van Looy a relatively free ride until it was time for him to sprint.

In 1977, there was still a Flandria team, they still wore red jerseys, and they were still working for one dominant leader. Flandria often rode in a high-speed formation to set up Freddy Maertens, the world champion. Sean Kelly turned professional for Flandria that year and after impressing in some early-season races was elevated to their elite squad for

Paris–Nice in March, where he was put to work for Maertens. Flandria's road captain, the man who called the shots during the races, organised the troops and generally shouted and bullied, was the intimidating Marc Demeyer.

The sergeant-major approach favoured by Demeyer was entirely necessary. As Kelly says: 'In a team with eight strong Belgians, you need someone to make sure they're not all pulling in different directions.'

Even when Flandria won, Demeyer was rarely entirely satisfied. If Kelly or one of the others completed his contribution towards the lead-out yet still had the strength to hang on to the finish with the bunch, he would berate them for not trying hard enough. 'If you have the legs to finish in the bunch, you have the legs to do a hundred metres more on the front,' he would say. Maertens was a much gentler soul and would offer thanks and encouragement, even if only restricted to a few words.

In the 1970s and 1980s, Kelly says, the sprint finishes were like the Wild West, lawless battles for supremacy with each sheriff's tenure often lasting no more than a day before someone else galloped into town and took charge. There were sometimes sprinters who endured a little longer. Maertens collected victories by the armful, including eight stages of the 1976 Tour de France, five of which were sprint wins, and a record thirteen stages of the following year's Vuelta a

España, the majority of them sprints. Peugeot occasionally pooled resources to work for their sprinter Jacques Esclassan and at the 1977 Tour the whole Bianchi team was dedicated to leading out their Belgian rider Rik Van Linden, although not with any success, it has to be said. There was nothing like the level of organisation or sophistication that would come later.

In those days, the riders wore baggy woollen jerseys that sagged around the waists when soaked in sweat, offering an inviting handful for a sprinter looking to move up or hold someone else back. 'A fair bit of that would go on if you could get away with it,' says Kelly of the dark arts of sprinting. Kelly was considered a fearless, sometimes reckless, sprinter by others but he was by no means the only one who threw his weight around. 'Sometimes it was a case of nudging someone to make sure they didn't shut the door on you,' he says, with glorious understatement. 'Sometimes you'd move across the road towards the barriers to make sure no one could get past, but you had to do it gradually. The *commissaires* would take a very dim view if you swerved across someone else's path. And yes, sometimes, you pulled the odd jersey before they could do it to you. If you see someone else getting away with the kamikaze tactics you're going to have a go yourself.'

In his sprinting heyday, Kelly was no stranger to being relegated for irregular riding. On one occasion during the Tour, he'd already reached his hotel before finding out he'd been stripped of victory and placed last in the bunch as a penalty for whatever misdemeanour he'd perpetrated.

Part of the reason for the roughhouse tactics was that there was no one team in control and each sprinter was operating more or less alone. If the bunch sprints at the Tour really were the Wild West, few of the chiefs could call on the help of a line of Indians, instead they were freelancers ducking and diving towards the line.

One of Kelly's major rivals in the early 1980s was the Belgian Eric Vanderaerden who, with his blond perm, was as glamorous as Kelly was gritty. They frequently came up against one another in sprint finishes and often things would boil over. At the Grand Prix de Fourmies, a small one-day race in northern France, one year they battled all the way to the line and carried it on afterwards. Kelly's retort to the Belgian's prolonged complaint was concise – just two words, the second of which was 'off' – and Vanderaerden saw red, aiming a kick at Kelly's nether regions. As he swung one leg, his standing foot and cleated cycling shoe slipped from under him, and he landed on his backside. At Reims during the 1985 Tour, the pair were so preoccupied with each other they handed the Frenchman Francis Castaing the biggest win of his career. They spent the closing few hundred metres bumping and pushing each other. They took this brawl on wheels from one side of the road to the other and both riders took a hand off the bars to shove the other. Vanderaerden and Kelly were relegated to last and second last. As Kelly says: 'When you have two cowboys trying to pull the same tricks, it's going to get out of hand every now and then.'

Every now and then, a team would get itself together to instil some order to the chaos. In 1987, the Dutch Superconfex team began working for their sprinter Jean-Paul van Poppel. At the Tour, Superconfex, who wore green and grey jerseys, massed at the front whenever there was a sprint finish and although van Poppel only won two stages he did also take *the* green jersey for the points competition. The following year, Superconfex set up van Poppel to win four stages at the Tour and they perhaps represent the genesis of the modern sprint lead-out train, although they would only mass at the front in the final five kilometres or so to set up the finish.

In the early 1990s, Djamolidine Abdoujaparov, the Uzbek sprinter so fast and occasionally crazy he was called the Tashkent Terror, could count on the support from teammates at a succession of squads, from Carrera to Lampre to Polti but the game-changer was the Italian Saeco squad in the middle of that decade.

In 1996, Saeco signed Mario Cipollini, already one of the fastest sprinters in the world, and hooked him up to their train. Saeco were the Italian equivalent of the TGV, seven or eight diesel engines with absolutely no room for passengers.

Between 1996 and 2001, Cipollini won twenty-two stages of the Giro d'Italia (more than half his record haul of forty-two) and nine stages of the Tour de France, all of them coming after a perfect lead-out from Saeco's Red Train.

Saeco's red train would take control of the bunch much further from the finish than any team had attempted before, they would wind the speed up so high that any breakaway riders would be powerless to prevent being sucked up. Saeco were a fleet of Lambrettas leading arguably the most charismatic and flamboyant rider of all time to the line, although Cipollini would probably prefer to think of himself as Julius Caesar, sitting majestically in his chariot, as his willing horses pulled him along.

Inspired by Saeco, other teams assembled their own trains, with varying degrees of success. Telekom, for Erik Zabel, and Fassa Bortolo for Alessandro Petacchi were two of the notably well-drilled units. But it wasn't until more than a decade after Saeco had defined the lead-out train that High Road, later Columbia, then HTC-Columbia, came up with a formation to take their crown.

* * *

I had a conversation the other day with someone who likes the mountain stages because
they are more *mano a mano* and the guys go
until they crack but, to be fair, mountain stages
are pretty much the opposite. Maybe in the old
days it was like that but nowadays, with everyone on their power meters, they are literally
time trialling but with everyone setting off at
the same time. It's actually the least tactical side
of cycling on the road right now. In terms of
racing, bunch sprinting is really the only discipline that still uses all the variables of cycling.

Mark Cavendish

* * *

Ask Cavendish what makes a great sprinter and the
answer is initially surprising – 'not me' – but on closer
examination probably accurate. In fact, take any of the
great sprinters of the recent three decades and there's no
typical external attribute that leaps out. Cipollini was
1m89cm and around 76 kilos at his peak. Cavendish is
1m75cm and around 69kg. Kittel is the same height as
Cipollini but at least another four kilos heavier. Robbie
McEwen, the Australian who won twelve stages in the
Tour between 1999 and 2007, is 1m71cm and 67kg.
So sprinters can be said to come in big and small pack-
ages. And then there are the sprinters in between.

What counts is the make-up of the muscles or, as Cavendish puts it, the perfect balance between fast- and slow-twitch muscle fibres. Slow-twitch fibres contract slowly but can keep going for a long time so are good for endurance, which helps them survive the distance of a typical Tour stage and cope with the mountains. Fast-twitch fibres contract quickly but tire quickly too. They are where the speed comes from.

The balance is necessary because if they had predominantly fast-twitch fibres, they'd be more suited to the intense speed of track sprinting; if they were predominantly slow-twitch, they'd be up there with the climbers in the mountains.

My journey to find out what makes a top sprinter tick, inevitably brings me back to Cavendish, and when we meet in a smart bistro near his home in Essex I'm hoping to unlock some of the secrets.

'Endurance cycling is anaerobic,' he says. 'Ninety per cent of road cyclists can't do the muscle damage that track sprinters do. Track sprinters, like Chris Hoy, go so deep, so aerobic, that they destroy their muscles, but they can't suffer for a long time like a road cyclist. Track sprinting is pain; road cycling is suffering. Being a road sprinter is suffering first but still being able to inflict that pain on yourself at the end. People think we're lazy, that we don't do a stroke of work until the last two hundred metres, but we have to get there first *then* be able to put out fifteen

hundred watts or whatever. Alex Dowsett, who is a
lead-out man for the Movistar team now, says he finishes his lead-out and is absolutely finished. He says:
"I can't understand how you manage to sprint after
that." The thing is, we're tired but we can still find
that acceleration when it matters.'

The idea that sprinters are somehow the work-shy
corner-cutters of the bunch is wide of the mark. 'On
a flat day, a sprinter has to be at the front the whole
day, then the pace winds up with fifty kilometres to go
and then they go deep in the sprint,' says Cavendish.
'Even if you don't win, you still go deep. It's not as if
it's easier if you finish second. On a rolling day, we
have to sit at the front even more so we have a buffer
on the hills, meaning we can drop back through the
bunch but not get dropped by the bunch. There's
more stress because there's a chance we might get over
the hills but there's no guarantees so it messes with
your mind. If we get dropped, we have to chase back
on in case there's a chance to sprint. On a mountain
stage, we're going as hard as the guys at the front,
probably more so. When they [the climbers and the
overall contenders] are riding easy at the front on the
first mountain of the day we're on the limit. We don't
get dropped that early but we're on the limit. After
that we have to ride hard enough to make it inside the
time cut, sometimes we're racing down the descents
and on the flat so hard. Even the time trials aren't an

easy day because if you step off the gas too much you could miss the time limit.'

Cavendish says that Team Sky's coach and sports scientist Tim Kerrison told him during the 2012 Tour: 'I find it harder to understand how you finish the Tour than I do understanding how Brad [Wiggins] can win it.

'Put me on a rig and you probably wouldn't even call me a sprinter,' he says. But draw a line across the road and it's like a switch has been flicked. 'You've got to be able to suffer, that's first, then there's something in your head, a desire . . . give me a sniff of the finish line and there's a winner's instinct, something that means you can switch things off and do things you didn't think were possible just because there's a line there.'

Kittel is just unbelievably strong. I duck and dive; Kittel is physically incredible. He's Ivan Drago [from *Rocky IV*]. He's not Dolph Lundgren [the actor who played the part], he's actually the character Ivan Drago.

Mark Cavendish

THE ANATOMY OF A SPRINT

In order for the sprinters to have a chance, the bunch has to arrive at the finish all together. That's a misleadingly simple way to sum up four, five or six hours of complex tactics, careful calculations and decision-making.

If we use the HTC-Columbia team as our case study, focusing on the last couple of years when they had polished their strategy as close to perfection as we're likely to see, we can look at some of the factors that contributed to setting up Cavendish.

Lars Bak, a Danish rider, was part of that team. Bak describes himself as a diesel perfectly suited to the job of towing the bunch along for hour after hour. On a flat stage of the Tour, his job began at kilometre zero. The first task was to allow a break to get away without creating a rod for his own back later on. That meant controlling the size of the breakaway and determining the size of the gap they were allowed to take.

When HTC-Columbia were at the peak of their powers in 2011, and Cavendish was at the peak of his, they found few willing allies in the peloton and so had to do the bulk of this grunt work themselves. Their rivals were not willing to tire themselves out to help set up another Cavendish win. Other teams might get involved in the final quarter of a stage but the heavy work was left to Bak and, often, just one or two team-mates. In the 2011 Tour, it was Bak and the American Danny Pate.

Knowing they would be short of help, the size of the breakaway was critical because: 'The maximum we could allow to go away was five riders. It wasn't that we were looking at who was going away, just the number. Three, four, five riders, we knew we could control,' says Bak.

It's a simple numbers game. Five committed riders in the break could be managed reasonably well by just two strong horses on the front of the bunch. Any more would be dangerous.

Usually there's a scrap to get into that break, particularly when places in the escape are so limited, and so the start of a stage can often see an hour of fast, aggressive, unpredictable racing until finally a suitable group is allowed to go clear. When they're happy with the composition of the break, they'll let it go, often by stopping for a pee.

By the time the bunch are back up to speed, the break has usually established a lead of four or five minutes.

The next important factor is limiting the break's advantage. With only a couple of riders to control the pace on the front of the bunch in 2011, Bak was nervous about letting any group gain more than three or four minutes.

It may surprise people to know that it is not necessarily the riders in the breakaway that are dictating matters. Instead, there's a delicate game of cat and mouse going on. The cat (the bunch) doesn't want to capture and kill the mouse until right near the end of the game, so he toys with it.

'We are deciding the speed the breakaway rides at,' says Bak.

If the break gets more time than the bunch would like, the bunch will speed up, forcing the leaders to either go harder – which would make them realise that they would tire too far from the finish and kill their already slim chances of surviving to the end, and so slow down a bit – or settle into a rhythm that suits the bunch.

'Sometimes the breakaway is bluffing you,' says Bak. 'We have to ride at a certain speed to make sure they get tired. We can look at our SRM [the handlebar-mounted computers which measure the power output, in the form of watts] and work out how hard they are going.'

This delicate balance is tricky to strike. Chase too hard and the break might give up, meaning that the whole process has to start again, which is far from ideal with the halfway mark of the stage approaching. Go too easily and the break might steal too great an advantage for relatively little effort, dramatically increasing their chances of staying clear and contesting the finish among themselves.

'Mentally, keeping it at three minutes breaks them,' says Bak. 'In the final twenty-five kilometres, the captains and leaders of all the teams want to come up [to the front, where it is safer, relatively speaking], the bunch is nervous and the speed is higher.'

This is when the break's advantage is hacked away in great chunks.

With ten kilometres to go, Bak and Pate would hand over to the lead-out train, which would have massed at the front behind them. The riders then take it in turns to keep the pace high. One man might have responsibility to ride from the ten-kilometre-to-go mark to five kilometres to go. As the finish gets closer, so the speed goes up and the turns taken at the front of the bunch shorten.

Meanwhile, other sprinters and their trains are trying to do the same thing and there's a tug-of-war-style battle for control at the front. Being on the front, fully in control of the bunch, has a number of advantages, the most important of which is that you can choose which line to take and which side of the road to use, depending on the type of corners, whether there are roundabouts and which direction the wind is blowing from.

The perfect, unopposed lead-out train would drop its leader off with around two hundred metres to go. In Cavendish's case, he would come off the wheel of his final lead-out man when he feels ready and before his teammate begins to tire and slow down, using the slipstream to full effect and picking the perfect moment to accelerate.

Of course, nothing goes perfectly to plan every time so while the blueprint is there to be followed, the riders must be flexible enough to adapt to the ever-changing circumstances around them.

> It looks easy on TV, so easy. It looks slow as well.
> I remember the last stage of the 2010 Ruta del
> Sol – I actually didn't finish that stage – we were
> watching it on the bus on the way to the airport.
> Mick Rogers won the race overall and Mark
> [Renshaw] was riding on the front with Mick
> behind. It looked so easy but Mark said: 'We
> were on the limit, absolutely killing ourselves.'
> No wonder people watch on TV and think it's
> like playing chess. These guys make it look easy.
>
> **Mark Cavendish**

While he's sitting on the wheel of his trusted lead-out man, Cavendish is watching and assessing everything that's going on around him, a bit like the cox in a rowing boat who's been given a set of oars.

This is where his forensic ability to read the race comes into play. He runs through a hypothetical finish: 'I know if I go from this position to that position, there's going to be a space opening up there, so I can go there, but that means that this person will move up there, so I could be boxed in . . . There's a space on the right but a team could come up that side, so I'd rather be on the left where there isn't room for them to come up that side . . .'

None of that imaginary conversation would be happening in his mind, instead it's an unconscious journey, as natural as it would be for you and me to drive to work for the thousandth time. We don't tell ourselves: 'Left here, right at the lights, right-hand lane at the roundabout otherwise that van will cut me up,' we just do it. Cavendish is making a series of decisions knowing the likely outcomes and eliminating the least desirable choices.

Dave Brailsford often says that Shane Sutton understands track racing at a different level to most people. 'Shane is watching in colour, the rest of us are watching in black and white,' he says. I suggest to Cavendish that his reading of a sprint finish is a bit like looking at a magic eye picture and seeing the image straight away.

'That's actually a good analogy,' he says. 'But I don't know why I do it, it's just something I do.'

I ask him if he finds it difficult to do nothing, either on the bus to and from the races, or in hotel rooms, or airport waiting rooms or at home. 'Yes. I think that's a trait of most driven sportspeople but of sprinters particularly. We don't rest, mentally. I do these puzzles, Hashi is the latest one . . .'

Cavendish talks me through a bewildering puzzle game that looks like sudoku on acid. It's a number puzzle and, from what I can gather, you can put some numbers in some circles but not in others and there's one definitive solution. I pay attention to start with but very quickly he loses me and I'm nodding politely, silently resolving to have a go at the puzzle later.

'I can't directly translate it to bike racing,' he says. 'I play chess but people said it helps me with tactics – it doesn't, but it's training the part of the brain that makes tactical decisions. The brain is a muscle and I try to train that part of it but it doesn't directly correlate to racing.'

* * *

If Mark Cavendish says that he is not necessarily the strongest physical specimen, what is it that has driven him to become arguably the greatest bunch sprinter ever, as *L'Équipe* said in 2012? It strikes me as too easy to say he's driven by a need or a desire to be the best.

I ask him about his childhood and, particularly, what he was like at school. 'I wasn't rough,' he says. 'We weren't working class, we weren't middle class. Me and my brother [Andy] had behavioural problems. I was all right because I was intelligent. Andy got in with the knobheads. You know there's always a guy at school who does boxing. He's okay, but there's always his followers who think they're boxers too. They do skipping in PE but they're not ripped, they're fat. Andy hung around with them. They thought they were streetwise but I could run circles round them.'

He paints the picture of a hyperactive child, quick to get bored if things weren't engaging him, even quicker with the back-chat and always ready with an answer. His mum Adele ran a dancewear shop and took him to dance lessons when he was a youngster and it is that, perhaps, which created the sportsman we know today.

Dancing is about discipline, the permanent pursuit of perfection, balance, poise and finesse, all skills that Cavendish has applied to cycling.

'It's embedded in us, this winning, this competitiveness,' he says about the small band of elite sprinters. 'It's what we have to do. At school sports day I had to win, if there was a spelling contest or a general knowledge quiz, I had to win.'

It's a familiar theme. The sporting superstar who wins because something deep inside him demands it, but it's more nuanced than that. 'I wasn't the best at everything. There were better runners than me. In the school football team everyone wanted to be the striker. I was as big at thirteen as I am now, I started puberty before everyone else, but in the football team I was the left-back. When I was younger, I could write pretty well with both hands, I could kick with both feet and I played left-back because there were no left-footers. I was happy with that, I was good at that and I could get praise for that.'

All the guys who win have a respect for each
other because we understand the pressure that
is on all of us to win. The second tier riders
– the ones who are third, fourth and fifth but
always third, fourth or fifth, never first – they
hate us and we hate them. They're reckless but
they think we're reckless. They think you can't
win without being reckless but we're not, we're
just better. There's a difference between putting
yourself in danger and putting others in danger. The top guys will put themselves in danger.

Mark Cavendish

THE PSYCHOLOGY OF A SPRINT

All the clichés about the *peloton* as it heads towards
a sprint finish have an element of truth about them.
The tension increases as the kilometres count down.
At the Tour riders are prepared to take more risks
than at other races, which is why the team or teams
controlling the pace at the front wind it up as fast as
possible to prevent the chancers from being able to
cause havoc. Sometimes the finish is like an obstacle
course with roundabouts and traffic islands. Studying
the official race handbook, which provides maps of
the final five kilometres, only goes so far. Sometimes
the detail is lacking and Cavendish will use Google
Street View to run through a finish. All the top teams

send someone ahead to drive or ride the final kilo-metres to report back with technical information. At HTC-Columbia, it was Erik Zabel, a six-time win-ner of the Tour de France's green jersey, who relayed that information and Cavendish trusted it implicitly. 'Experience told me Erik was never wrong. His eye for detail and mine are the same. I can do a lap of a circuit and straight away tell you where all the potholes are. The way he talked about a sprint gave me confidence. If he said: "There's a ninety-degree corner, you can't see round it but don't brake because you can go full gas," I'd go round the corner full gas and everybody else would brake. He was never wrong, he could feel the sprints.'

There is only a handful of people who can teach Cavendish about sprinting. One is his teammate Mark Renshaw, who was rated as the best lead-out man in the world when he was at HTC-Columbia, then struck out on his own, with limited success, at the Dutch Rabobank team, before rejoining Cavendish at Omega Pharma-Quick Step in 2014. The other is Alessandro Petacchi, who also joined up with Cavendish at Omega Pharma. 'We'd get on the bus and I'd listen to Mark talk about the sprints and he always said something that I thought "yeah, you're right". I would take Mark's judgement of the move-ment in the peloton every time. I would follow his wheel and trust him. Tactically he is incredible. And

Petacchi is the only one who has beaten me and I've thought: "He's studied me." At the Giro d'Italia in 2009, at Trieste, he jumped early and caught me out and he realised that I was leaving it later and later, I'd got a bit lazy maybe, but he worked out how to beat me even though I was physically in the best form I'd ever been in.'

It is interesting that Cavendish, the obsessive with an eye for detail that borders on control freakery, allows himself to trust others to such an extent.

'I am pretty loud and aggressive in the run-up to the sprint, from thirty kilometres to go to ten kilometres to go. When we're trying to get control of it I'll shout quite a bit. I am quite stressed then, that's the most nerve-racking part because if we make mistakes there, it can cost us later,' he says. 'That's the thing about sprinting, people watch one sprint and try to work out why this person won but in the Tour, something that happened earlier that day, such as the bunch going hard over a particular climb, can have a knock-on effect. In fact something that happened four days earlier can have an effect. And that's why it's so stressful in those last thirty kilometres because that's the point where we can take control.'

Cavendish has been quoted as saying he hates losing with a passion so I ask him what he hates most: losing or making mistakes?

'Making mistakes. You look at details to make

you better, but I look at the details to stop failure. I can do that for myself but it's hard to do with other people. Rod [Ellingworth, the former British Cycling academy coach] had a go at me because I used to get frustrated that not everyone thinks like me.'

So that phase of the race, the twenty or so kilometres before the last ten, is where Cavendish feels least in control, which perhaps explains why he is so vocal and on edge.

But once the race reaches the final ten kilometres, he describes a period of calm where the subconscious takes over. His brain is processing information, making decisions and predicting outcomes. The level of concentration and physical strain combines to produce a violent explosion in the last 200 metres of a sprint.

The mental stress at the Tour is what hooks you. The Giro is physically tiring and you can be on your knees but it's not the same. The Tour is all emotional stress. It's the only race where you have the 200 best guys, all in peak condition, all with real consequences of winning and losing – career-changing, life-changing consequences. Watch the peloton in the Tour and you'll see how short it is compared to the Giro. It's squashed up because everyone wants to be near the front.

Everyone is riding so close together, touching
elbows. Then you've got the media circus that
goes on every day and it knocks you.

Mark Cavendish

When the sprinters cross the line they go from sixty to
zero in seconds, not just physically but mentally too.
The elation of winning or the anger at losing has to go
somewhere and that is when the riders are squeezed
into the bottleneck, swarmed around by journalists
and television crews. It takes a while to return to earth.

'There's no other sport in the world where you
come off the pitch and suddenly they're asking
questions over each other. You can't process it,' says
Cavendish. 'When you've won a race, for us that's
like scoring a goal, but in a football match when the
guy's celebrating they don't go and ask him how it
feels right at that moment. When I was younger one
of the things I loved about cycling was how close the
fans got, how close everyone can get to the riders and
you can see that emotion close up, but sometimes it
goes too far. You can argue that we're paid to do the
job but we're still human beings.'

The release after the finish line is immense. The
brain has been suspended in a peculiarly false state
of calm during a hectic, dangerous and unpredictable
period of fifteen minutes. Something has to give.

'It has to. You can't hold it back. When you win,

it's elation, ecstasy, when you lose, you're livid. That's going to come out one way or another and you can't just bottle it up a few seconds later.'

* * *

During Cavendish's era of dominance, particularly from 2009 to 2011, people began to hope that a credible rival would emerge to make things more interesting but that, perhaps, reveals that the technical intrigue of the sprints is difficult to grasp and understand. I remember speaking to Cavendish after a stage he'd won and he was in a spiky mood. 'Did you watch the race?' he asked. I said that I had and I made a point about a move the Garmin team had made in the final five kilometres and wondered whether that had been decisive. 'That had nothing to do with it,' he said, before explaining the significance of something else that I hadn't seen and probably wouldn't have recognised as important even if I had.

Seeking to understand a Tour de France sprint without having experienced it is very difficult and so it becomes a matter of subjective interpretation. In the binary world of modern sport, where wins and losses seem to count more than at any time before, it would be a shame to abandon the quest to understand.

The beauty of bunch sprinting is obvious. There's the speed, the danger, the unpredictability. Like

boxing's heyday when there was only one heavyweight
champion of the world, there can only be one fastest
man on earth. We watch on the edge of our seats, as
they power towards the line, we gasp when they duck
and weave and we wince when they crash. Yes, it's all
about winning and losing but there is more to this
complex art than who crosses the line first. It would
be like choosing the heavyweight boxing world champion by nothing more than measuring who has the
hardest punch.

Lionel Birnie is co-founder of *The Cycling Anthology*. He
first covered the Tour de France in 1999 and was the *Sunday
Times* correspondent when Bradley Wiggins won it in 2012.
He published Sean Kelly's autobiography *Hunger*, which was
shortlisted for Irish Sports Book of the Year, and is co-host of
The Cycling Podcast.

4

To a generation of promising British, Irish and Australian riders, the Athletic Club de Boulogne-Billancourt was the gateway to a professional career.

Based in an unremarkable street in the west of Paris, the club had a reputation for nurturing the best. If you could make it at ACBB, you could make it anywhere.

James Startt tells the story of the *acébébistes* and asks how a club that produced Stephen Roche, Robert Millar and Phil Anderson, among others, suddenly fell out of love with English-speaking riders.

INSIDE THE PARISIAN
DREAM FACTORY

BY JAMES STARTT

PARIS, FRANCE

The old clubhouse on Rue de Sèvres has long closed down and the team apartments reconverted into private housing. And the lustre has more than faded around the current clubhouse on Rue Yves Kermen, planted ignominiously in the shadows of a Bricorama, a low-cost home supply supermarket on the outskirts of Boulogne-Billancourt, itself a suburb of Paris.

Only the sign over the archway reading *Complexe Jacques Anquetil* hints at a more glorious past, as does a small selection of trophies on show in the window.

Once inside the current clubhouse of the Athletic Club de Boulogne-Billancourt, the discerning eye will notice other remnants of the club's zenith. There is the white jersey with red polka dots awarded to the best climber in the Tour de France. Made of wool, it dates back to 1984, when one of the club's protégés, a certain Robert Millar, became the first Scot to capture such a prize. And then there is a yellow jersey from the Tour de France. Made of nylon and sporting the Carrera team's logo on the chest, it belonged to Ireland's Stephen Roche, the last of the club's alumni to go on and win the Tour de France in 1987.

In its prime years during post-war France, the Athletic Club de Boulogne-Billancourt, more commonly known as l'ACBB rose to prominence as the country's pre-eminent sports club, boasting Olympic champions in an array of sports.

But it was in bicycle racing where the club left its biggest mark, producing Tour de France champions such as Jean Robic, Jacques Anquetil, the first five-time winner, or Bernard Thévenet, himself a two-time winner.

In the 1970s and 1980s the club unwittingly encouraged the transformation of bicycle racing in Europe. The club ushered in the first great anglophone invasion and the sport's days as an almost exclusively European pursuit were over.

Not that the club's motivation was particularly visionary. It wasn't. They weren't necessarily interested in revolutionising cycling, or offering opportunities to foreign riders, they were simply interested in maintaining their position at the top of the annual ranking of amateur clubs in France. ACBB fielded the *crème de la crème* of British, Irish and Australian talent, helping to develop the best of them into the most respected professionals of their generation.

Leading the initiative was the cycling club's general

manager Paul Wiegant, known to everyone as Mickey. Wiegant was a dapper director who, after consolidating the club's supremacy in the 1960s with stars such as André Darrigade, Jean Stablinski and Jacques Anquetil, then expanded beyond the frontiers of France in the 1970s.

His moniker, apparently given to him because he wore a Mickey Mouse patch on his jersey during his formative years as a track racer, reflected an uncharacteristic detour of frivolity to his otherwise exacting demeanour.

'Monsieur Wiegant was truly old school,' says one long-standing member of ACBB. 'You always called him "Monsieur Wiegant". He would tell you what clothes to wear for dinner and if your elbow was on the table, he would knock it off with a knife. And in a race he was even capable of shutting down a breakaway with four of our riders in it, just because the "right" rider was not in it.'

For many, Wiegant's club was nothing less than a university for cycling, and the team's results far surpassed even those of the French national amateur team.

Through his strong ties with the town of Boulogne-Billancourt he was able to secure housing where riders from the provinces or foreigners could live and his ties to the legendary Peugeot professional team allowed ACBB to serve as a feeder club, offering the best riders the opportunity to graduate to the professional ranks in a seamless manner.

The first British rider to do so was Paul Sherwen, who raced for the club in 1977 and turned professional in 1978. But Sherwen preferred to sign with the rival Fiat team. Before leaving, however, he recommended his friend Graham Jones to ACBB. Jones won prestigious amateur Classics such as Paris–Troyes and Paris–Évreux as well as the Grand Prix des Nations time trial while riding for ACBB and became the first British rider to graduate from ACBB to Peugeot.

After Sherwen and Jones, the floodgates opened. The clubhouse doors opened to Scotland's Robert Millar and London-born Australian Phil Anderson in 1979, Dubliner Stephen Roche in 1980, British riders Sean Yates and John Herety in 1981, Australian Allan Peiper in 1982 and Ireland's Paul Kimmage in 1984.

Graduates of the Paris club were known as '*acébébistes*' and the anglophones were called, collectively, the Foreign Legion. Anderson held the yellow jersey at the Tour de France for two spells, Roche won the Giro d'Italia, Tour de France and World Championships in 1987, Millar became one of the best climbers in Europe and Peiper and Yates were respected *domestiques*. The club's reputation for recruiting talent from previously untapped areas and developing them into riders to rival the best France could produce was confirmed.

For a handful of anglophone riders, it was possible

to turn professional without ACBB, as Ireland's Sean Kelly and the Americans Jock Boyer and Greg LeMond proved, but for many the most direct route was through the doors of the ground-breaking Parisian club.

Although ACBB ushered in a wave of foreign riders, Monsieur Wiegant had no global vision for cycling. No, he was far too much the Machiavellian. Results were all that mattered to him, and this band of rag-amuffin riders proved to be the perfect mercenaries.

'Wiegant was looking for good riders and that's all,' says Jean-Claude Le Dissez, one of the club's sec-retaries at the time. 'It was just about results. Wiegant liked the foreign riders because they didn't ask ques-tions. They were just there to ride.'

On the face of it, the ACBB squad left little to be desired, even when compared to some professional teams. Known as '*les petits gris*' for their distinctive orange and grey jerseys, they were sponsored by one of France's top automobile and bicycle producers and showed up to each race with Peugeot bikes as well as team cars.

But seen from the inside, the foreign riders soon learned another reality: that of a heartlessly competi-tive system where only victory won you the respect of Wiegant or his top *directeur sportif*, Claude Escalon.

'Someone was supposed to meet me at the airport and take me to the training camp. But when I arrived there was no one to meet me,' says Stephen Roche of his arrival in France. 'There were no mobile phones at that time, but I had the address for the clubhouse so I took a cab to Rue de Sèvres. The cab arrived at the bottom of the one-way street and the driver pointed and said, "The clubhouse is up that way."

'I got out of the car and dragged my suitcase up the street. It was late, though, and of course everything was closed when I got there so I just jumped over the gates, hid my bags behind the bushes and went off to try and find a meal. Afterwards I returned, got my bag from the bushes and just slept on the porch.

'Then the next morning at about 5 a.m. two guys stopped by. They were on their way from Lille down to the training camp on the Côte d'Azur.

'They opened the gates and said, "Are you Roche?"

'"Yes," I said. And they said, "Come with us."

'I climbed into the back of a Peugeot 104 and sixteen hours later I was in the south of France. That was my welcome to France.'

Riders who joined the club before and after Roche tell a virtual carbon-copy tale of their own arrival in Paris, so much so that many suspect the botched rendezvous was an unspoken litmus test for the new boys.

'I took the overnight bus from Victoria station [in London] to Gare du Nord,' remembers Sean Yates, who followed in Roche's footsteps. 'They said that they would have someone to meet me but there was no one. I reckon it was a way of seeing how tough you

were because some of the foreign riders had a reputation for being a bit soft, and some went home after a
couple of weeks. So if you passed that first test they
really liked that.'

Once in France, riders were quickly shown their
lodging before being shipped to southern France for
the team's first early-season training camp – and, as
was often the case, further testing.

'They would ship everybody to the Côte d'Azur
for the early training races like the Grand Prix of St
Tropez,' says Neil Martin, a member of the class of
1979, and father of Garmin-Sharp's Tour de France
stage winner, Daniel. 'Basically it was a test area. There
were about forty of us down there and it was only
when we got there that we found out that only twenty-two were going to race for the rest of the year. After
a week or so you just didn't see some guys any more.

Martin is one of many who did not 'make it' with
ACBB. A roommate of Anderson's, Martin raced consistently well. As an eighteen-year-old he won one of
the early-season races but at the end of his first season
he was not invited back for another.

'We were the best club in France. Even guys like
Jacques Anquetil knew that it was with us that they
had their best chance to pro,' says Charles Desorbaix,
a card-carrying 'acébébiste' since 1948. Today, he is
the senior member of the club and still accompanies
juniors on the Wednesday afternoon training outings

in the nearby Longchamps Hippodrome. 'The foreigners that came here were really serious. They were all scared that they would get sent back if they weren't. And they knew that they had one season to prove themselves,' he says.

Victory, the riders also learned early on, was the only thing that mattered at ACBB and for some of the foreigners, winning was the only way they'd make enough money to eat.

Unlike many of their French teammates, they received no monthly stipend. In essence, they understood, they were racing in exchange for their equipment and the rent on the apartments at 110 Rue de Bellevue. Extra money for food would, on occasion, be paid as an advance against future prize earnings. But there was no free lunch.

Yet while the terms of employment were austere at best, the foreign riders largely accepted them without question. They understood that ACBB offered the most direct path to the professional ranks, something that only a few years earlier would have been nothing more than a pipe dream.

For most riders, the move to ACBB was a considerable step up. Australian Allan Peiper came to the French club after three years racing in Belgium, where his accommodation was simply some space in the local butcher shop. By comparison, the two-bedroom flats ACBB provided in Boulogne were extravagant.

'The apartments were actually very nice. We had beautiful bikes and a great kit,' Peiper recalls. 'But a lot of times I was in the apartment by myself. I was just completely isolated. I didn't have any money. The hardest thing was finding and paying for food. I remember one day there was a choice between half a baguette and a yogurt or half a baguette and some apples. I had to make the choice of eating two things and not three because I didn't have any money.'

Sean Yates apparently ate better than Peiper as he made himself quite useful as a lead-out man to sprinter John Herety in the week-night *nocturne* criteriums. The two would then split the primes for food money.

With victory such a commodity, the newcomers often found themselves at odds with French teammates, who could often be tougher rivals than riders from other clubs. After all, they were all fighting for the same spots on a professional team the following year, and by the early 1980s some French riders must have felt like they were submitting to an anglophone invasion. The first riders to join ACBB, Sherwen and Jones, may have been viewed by the locals as oddities, but with the stunning success of Anderson, Millar and Roche, the foreign riders were soon seen as direct rivals to the French.

'I remember racing in the Franco–Belge race,' Peiper says. 'It was a race that if you won it you turned pro. I was in the leader's jersey on the final day. We hit the final circuit and the team car was not allowed to follow. And I punctured. All my teammates just stopped. They just pulled out. Finally I got a wheel from a tourist on the side of the road. I caught the peloton and went to the front, because the second and third-place riders went up the road when I punctured. I chased and chased, but I lost the leader's jersey by one second. My teammates let me down. But you know they just really didn't give a shit.'

But it is hard to deter oddballs with unfavourable odds. The foreigners that made it through ACBB not only had to be outstanding bike riders, but fiercely independent and self-sufficient at a very young age. For many, the heart of their education came on the road.

The world, it is often said, is a smaller place today because of telecommunications, the Internet and the ease of travel. But it appeared far different in the 1970s and early 1980s. Those leaving home to race in France could not count on Facebook, email or a mobile phone to keep in touch with friends or family on a daily basis. Instead they had to go weeks or months without even a phone call. And while the astute traveller can find the airfare from England to France for less than a hundred euros today, back then it could cost four times more. There was, of course, no channel tunnel linking Paris and London by rail, and the ferry was out unless a rider could get from the capital to Calais by train.

But if those coming from England were making a huge leap, riders from Australia had to make a comparative interstellar journey to arrive in France. Only the toughest – or those who, like Yates, admitted to being 'a bit of a loner' – survived.

Coming to France required a huge personal investment and the riders that endured the adventure never lost sight of what motivated them to make the journey in the first place: a shot at reaching the pro ranks. Likewise, many of the lessons learned at ACBB would help them further down the road if they did earn a professional contract.

'They develop a sense of responsibility when they leave their countries to seek their fortunes here,' said Maurice De Muer, *directeur sportif* of the Peugeot professional team in an article headlined 'A Little English on the Tour', by Samuel Abt, that was published in the *International Herald Tribune* in July 1981. 'The only choice they have is to do well or go home. [Phil] Anderson was so eager to make good he even cut his long hair!'

From the start of the 1980 season Stephen Roche had performed tremendously for ACBB, winning many early season races as well as the first major amateur Classic of the year, Paris–Ezy. He was also a regular visitor to the podium but, when he asked whether his results would stand him in good stead when it came to getting a professional contract, Wiegant was dismissive of all his results bar the victories. He told Roche matter-of-factly: 'It is not second and third places that get pro contracts.'

Roche responded two days later by winning the amateur Paris–Roubaix. 'I'll never forget in the final I was with the Belgian Dirk Demol. The ACBB car had a broken window during the race, but Wiegant was leaning out yelling, "Roche, if you don't win here you're going home!"'

The next night, Roche rang his boss at the engineering company where he worked as a maintenance fitter, and said: 'I've just won the biggest amateur Classic. I'm not coming back.'

The jealousy may have run deep with some of the French riders but they could not deny that the foreign riders were getting results.

'A chain of similarly gutsy riders came through ACBB,' says Australian journalist Rupert Guinness, author of *The Foreign Legion*, a history of anglophone riders who went to mainland Europe, mostly France, in the 1980s. 'Wiegant liked them. He saw that they were willing to have a go and attack and, whether it was their bravado, or that the French riders didn't know them, they got results.'

According to Jean-François Oléon, one of the French riders at the time: 'They were just hungrier!' A top junior in France, Oléon was recruited by Wiegant as a first-year senior in 1980 and has remained a life-long friend of Roche. 'They had a fighting spirit 24 hours a day and they didn't ask questions. They weren't going to complain if their shorts or jersey didn't fit quite right. That wasn't always the case with us French riders.'

Jean-François Guiborel, another French amateur who was not hostile to the newcomers remembers mostly the sheer talent or *classe* that the foreigners all seemed to possess. 'I don't know how he did it but Wiegant just found one good rider after the next. They were all good, just so good.'

In reality, the golden age of English-speaking riders at ACBB was relatively short. Sherwen was there in 1977 and in 1986 Paul Kimmage was the last notable rider to turn professional, although he spent a year with CC Wasquehal after leaving ACBB. But in a short period of time these riders left an indelible mark. This Parisian club suddenly had international cachet because so many of them had notable professional careers.

Wiegant, perhaps aware of the potential of certain riders, was known to have his favourites. On occasion he was even known to loosen his iron grip, inviting selected riders to stay at his house in the south of France to prepare for the early season races or a particular objective. Roche, Yates and Peiper all benefited from Wiegant's hospitality and Peiper attributes his late-season Grand Prix des Nations time trial victory to a stay at Wiegant's, one filled with two training rides a day and motor-paced sessions.

More often than not, the riders that excelled under Wiegant's watch at ACBB went on to excel in the professional ranks.

'Oh yeah, they really stood out,' says Samuel Abt, himself one of the pioneering anglophone journalists in cycling and a veteran of thirty-one Tours de France. '*L'Équipe* had stories about them all the time. They were so different. Nobody had seen so many anglophone riders and they just sort of burst on the scene. And this was way before there were any Eastern Europeans. Daniel Mangeas [the Tour de France's official speaker] could never pronounce their names. Guys like Anderson and Roche were doing very well at the start. It was a new wave.'

While the Foreign Legion left its mark on professional cycling in the 1980s and clearly helped pave the road for the international sport that cycling is today, Abt avoids saying that the anglophone presence in the peloton was prescient. 'It was just a handful of guys sprinkled around. We didn't get the sense really that the times were changing. There weren't that many of them. But it was extraordinary because the sport was so European. No, it wasn't even European. The sport up until then was just so French, Belgian and Italian.'

Within years, the empire that Wiegant built unravelled. Peugeot began to gradually withdraw from cycling in 1986 and the town of Boulogne-Billancourt appeared less interested in the foreign aspect of their club, perhaps because the flood of talent was waning. Yet by all standards it had been an exceptional run.

For those that shared the common but unique experience that was ACBB there are few regrets. Most feel that they were the fortunate ones to be part of something truly special at a time when the sport was showing its first hints of change as the sport was taking its first tentative steps towards being truly international.

'It was a great schooling. Even outside of sports it was just a great education,' Roche says without hesitation. 'By 1982 standards it was avant-garde,' says Peiper.

Even Neil Martin, who, like the majority of *stagiaires*, did not make it to the professional ranks with the club, admits that the ACBB experience was 'a proper grounding. I was always proud that I was part of it'.

It also provided some long-term dividends. 'You know my son Dan had a very similar year to myself starting out at Vélo Club La Pomme in Marseille,' Martin says. 'That's the ACBB of today with, what, twenty-seven guys turning pro in six years. But it was pretty rudimentary, with six guys in an apartment for three. What ACBB gave me was a complete understanding of what he was going through and I think that possibly helped him because anything he was going through I had experienced. He was eighteen, exactly the same age as I was when I left. But he survived. And they are looking for the survivors.'

Dan Martin of course has done better than survive and after winning Liège–Bastogne–Liège as well as a stage in the Tour de France in 2013, the Irishman is seen as one of the peloton's top talents. But while his success, like that of Sir Bradley Wiggins, Cadel Evans or Chris Froome, continues to forge new territory for British, Irish and Australian riders, these riders are not packaged into a specific group the way the Foreign Legion were. Today their numbers are simply too great for them to be considered an oddity or an anomaly. Some might even say that the invaders have taken over.

James Startt will cover his twenty-fifth Tour de France in 2014, making him the senior American journalist in the Tour de France press room. Startt is the author of *Tour de France/Tour de Force* (Chronicle Books, 2000), the first history of the Tour de France in English. He has served as *Bicycling* magazine's Man in Europe, since 1999.

5

Matt Stephens refused to give up on a dream that was born on Alpe d'Huez – to become a pro rider.

He rode at the World Championships and the Olympic Games but the professional contract did not materialise, so he spent the prime of his career racing for small teams in Britain.

Then the Linda McCartney team offered him a chance to ride the 2000 Giro d'Italia. Given how long he had waited to achieve his ambition, it's understandable that he refused to throw in the towel when he suffered a terrible crash.

THE CRASH

BY MATT STEPHENS

The memory of the moment remains in glorious High Definition. It was 1986 and I was standing on Alpe d'Huez waiting for the Tour de France to arrive. We'd travelled to the Alps in Dad's brown Renault 4, which given its habit of breaking down made it an epic road trip in itself. I was a skinny sixteen-year-old looking forward to my first glimpse of the Tour. I was so thin, in fact, that although my mum had taken in my Lycra cycling shorts, they still flapped loosely around my thighs and had to be held up with clip-on braces. A knotted hanky on the head completed the look.

After all the waiting, the moment was magical. It was the day that Bernard Hinault and his teammate Greg LeMond, the best two riders in the race, broke clear of everyone else and, having set aside their rivalry at last, rode together on Alpe d'Huez. Hinault had won the Tour five times but as they approached I could not take my eyes off LeMond.

I doubt he remembers the moment as clearly as I do but I'm sure I looked into LeMond's blue eyes

– sunken through the pain and concentration yet still
somehow sparkling – as he powered past.

And that was it. The moment I decided I wanted
to do this.

* * *

Back home in Bushey, Hertfordshire, I got serious. I
sent off to the British Cycling Federation for a racing
licence, determined to one day make it as a professional racer. In late 1986, I joined the Hemel
Hempstead CC and would ride over there to do the
Sunday club runs and, the following summer, the
evening ten-mile time trials. Where once I had been a
cyclist, now I saw myself as a racing cyclist and there
was a big difference between the two.

My first-ever race was at the Eastway circuit in east
London, not far from where the Olympic velodrome
is now. I couldn't get my foot into the toe clips so
I got dropped straight away and rode round on my
own. The sight of my dad with his head in his hands
is burned into the memory.

Fortunately things improved and I turned out to
be pretty good. In 1988, I won the national junior
road race series, named the Peter Buckley Trophy after
the 1966 Commonwealth Games champion from the
Isle of Man, who was killed in a training accident
when in his mid-twenties. That meant I was one of

the best young riders in the country but I knew I had
to go to France eventually. At the time this was the
generally accepted path – actually, no, the only path
– to a professional career. I had options at the end of
1988, when I was due to make the transition from
junior to senior, but I decided to stay at home for one
more year. There were stories of many young British
riders who had shone as a junior but had been utterly
at sea in their first year racing against men, unable to
adapt to the longer distances and faster speed.

Back then, there were three categories of racing
cyclist. You were either a junior (aged eighteen and
under), an amateur or a professional. The amateur
category could be men against boys. There were some
tough competitors, riders who were almost good
enough to be professional but had not made the
step for whatever reason. The gulf in class could be
intimidating. In 1996, the governing body, the UCI,
recognised the situation and changed the system,
introducing the under-23 category as a stepping stone
from junior ranks to the professional or elite class.

I decided to give myself the best possible chance of
keeping my head above water when I eventually went
to France by staying at home for my first senior season, in 1989, to acclimatise. I could adjust in familiar
surroundings and make the occasional trip abroad
with the Great Britain team.

However, I needn't have been overly concerned. I

adapted remarkably well to the senior ranks and my naturally aggressive racing style and seemingly endless endurance helped me to a string of top places in the biggest British races. I still couldn't sprint for toffee, though, so wins weren't as regular as they might have been.

In the summer, I was selected for the Great Britain amateur team for the World Championship road race in Chambéry, France. I can still remember telling a journalist I was 'over the moon' to be picked. The clichés had started already.

Before the Worlds, the Great Britain team headed to Germany for the Hessen Rundfahrt, a seven-day stage race, as preparation. I climbed incredibly strongly all week – being nine stone wet through helped – and I won overall. I had a great bunch of older, more experienced teammates who helped me cope with the draining effect of defending the yellow jersey. The win was significant. (I didn't realise the significance at the time, but the winner the previous year had been a Russian rider called Pavel Tonkov, who went on to win the Giro d'Italia in 1996.) I had beaten all the top amateur riders from France, Spain, Germany and the other top nations and I also learned more about the subtleties and nuances of bike racing in those seven days than I had in all of my nascent career to that point. I have to mention my teammates Dave Cook and Steve Farrell for their work driving the pace on the front of the bunch, and Brian Smith for his tactical expertise and guidance.

Despite the experience, the World Championship road race the following month was a baptism of fire. We had to cover ten laps of a sixteen-kilometre course, which had a five-kilometre climb each lap with an average gradient of 10 per cent. I felt so sluggish the first time up the climb I was convinced my back brake was rubbing on my wheel. I stopped, got off my bike and span the back wheel to check. It was fine, no rubbing at all. 'Shit,' I thought. 'This is just a very fast race.'

Later on in the race, I punctured and any slim hope of getting a result disappeared. I finished twenty minutes behind the winner. My first World Championships had hurt but I'd loved every painful minute.

The day after our amateur race, I took my place among the thousands of fans to watch the professionals. The rain turned it into one of the most epic World Championship races of modern times. Who should win? Greg LeMond, the American who had won that 1986 Tour de France and had added his second title a few weeks earlier.

Nothing had changed for me. I still wanted to be one of them. If anything, my desire had deepened and was now an all-consuming passion.

***

Everything was going to plan. At the start of 1990, I headed across the channel to join a French amateur club. And not just any old club, but the best amateur club. I had been offered a place at the famous ACBB, the Athletic Club de Boulogne-Billancourt on the outskirts of Paris.

The ACBB had been home to a string of top English-speaking riders, Paul Sherwen, Phil Anderson, Robert Millar, Sean Yates and, most famously of all, the Irishman Stephen Roche, who won the Giro d'Italia, Tour de France and World Championships in 1987. ACBB was virtually a feeder club to the professional Peugeot squad. A place there did not guarantee a professional contract at the end of it, perhaps, but it offered a great chance. This was like earning a place at the Oxford or Cambridge of cycling.

The team was based in Boulogne-Billancourt, about ten kilometres from Versailles. My home for the next three years would be a converted police station, my room was a converted cell, complete with barred windows. We got 100 francs a month to cover our food expenses, so I quickly became a very shrewd shopper. I also learned French quickly because the team manager, Claude Escalon, refused to speak English.

My aim was simply to *passé pro* – turn professional – and so I lived the life of a tracksuited monk. Over the three years riding in the orange and grey colours of ACBB, I picked up one big win a season in the French Mavic Cup events, which were a big deal for the club, but I wasn't an out-and-out winner. My lack of a sprint finish meant I was never prolific. And in the amateur ranks, winning grabs the attention far more than a handful of second, third or fourth places.

My time at ACBB also coincided with a steep economic downturn. Sponsors were pulling out of professional cycling and there were fewer French teams. The Berlin Wall had come down, meaning there were riders from Eastern Europe, as well as Australia, America and Scandinavia all competing for the same places. I had matured well as a rider and I had the physical attributes but there were other riders, particularly French riders, winning more races than me.

In 1992, my third year with ACBB, I knew it was now or never. The club would be unlikely to keep me on for a fourth year. You either turned professional or you went home.

I was selected to ride the Olympic Games in Barcelona – the proudest moment of my career at that point. I was in great form and I wanted to ride well and catch someone's eye. I rode a solid race but I missed the key move and then got caught behind a crash in the final kilometre.

However, when I got back to Paris, the boss at ACBB told me the club was turning pro and that in

1993 we'd no longer be an amateur outfit, we'd be a pro team, sponsored by a Spanish dairy. It appeared that my determination was about to pay off. It wasn't one of the big French teams I'd dreamed of joining but it was another step up so I headed home for winter ready for a new challenge.

***

When the phone rang at home in late December 1992, I was surprised to hear my French team manager Claude Escalon on the other end, speaking to me for the first time in English. This was very odd indeed. He clearly wanted to make sure there was no confusion in translation. It wasn't good news. The Spanish dairy had pulled out and the pro team project was dead in the water. ACBB was reverting to the amateur ranks, but at a lower status than before and with a quarter of the funding. There was no place for me. I was distraught but I refused to accept that it was the end. I was still only twenty-two.

For the next couple of years, I raced in Britain and rode abroad for the national team. I wanted to ensure a certain standard of living, so I got a full-time job at Marks and Spencer, and scheduled my racing and training around that. It was a compromise, but one I had to make.

My belief had not wavered at all. I still knew I was

good enough to make it as a professional cyclist, I just found myself taking an unorthodox route. My training sessions were riding to and from work and spending hours riding at high intensity on my battered old turbo trainer in the garage. I had to ride hard whenever I got the chance because the opportunities to put in long training rides during the week were few and far between.

I struck a good balance and I was still a force on the British racing scene. In late summer 1995, I was selected for the British amateur team for the World Championships, which were to be held at altitude in Colombia.

The 1995 amateur World Championships were unusual because they were the qualification event for the 1996 Olympic Games in Atlanta, which would be open to professional riders for the first time. I knew someone from our team had to finish in the top thirty or else there would not be a British rider in the road race at the Atlanta Olympics. Considering the hilly course, that was not a given.

Because earning an Olympic place was so crucial, we had a couple of weeks' altitude training in Colorado before heading down to Colombia. I took a month's unpaid leave from Marks and Spencer to give myself the best possible chance.

I trained extremely hard in Colorado and the weight dropped off me. I was already light but I got down to sixty-six kilograms and I was dropping my

teammates on the climbs and feeling very strong. I
was also coping well with the effects of altitude.

The race went almost perfectly. I got into the winning ten-man move that went clear on only the second
lap. In hindsight I worked far too hard to establish
our lead but I sensed this was a great opportunity.
Behind us, there wasn't what you could call a *peloton.* The bunch had been shattered to pieces before
the halfway mark because of the hellish nature of the
course. We did ten laps of the sixteen-kilometre circuit, which gained 330 metres in elevation. It was the
hardest circuit I've ever raced on. The main climb was
six kilometres long and very steep in places.

As we began the penultimate lap, the strength in
my legs began to ebb away, although I was not the
only one. On the climb, our group split as we each
tackled the gradient at our own pace, urged on by
thousands of screaming Colombians. There were only
five Europeans in the leading group – the eventual
winner, Danny Nelissen of the Netherlands, a couple
of Italians, a Dane and me – the rest were Colombian,
Ecuadorian and Venezuelans who were used to racing
at altitude and the demands of the course.

I still find it hard to recall much about the final
couple of laps because they were ridden through
a haze of fatigue but I do remember being alone,
riding as hard as I could, unsure where exactly I was
on the road. I knew I was near the front but I didn't

know how many were in front of me.

As I crossed the line Doug Dailey, the Great Britain team manager, ran alongside me, his arm across my shoulders, face beaming, and shouted: 'Well done, lad, you've finished eighth in the world!'

I was so drained I couldn't say a word but I thought to myself 'That's all right.'

I was the only British rider to finish and, as a result, Great Britain qualified a team for the Atlanta Olympics, where Max Sciandri won a bronze medal in the road race. I later rode with Max on the Linda McCartney team and joked that without me he wouldn't have that medal at all.

Afterwards, as I was congratulated by my teammates and the staff, I thought: 'Surely that'll get me a pro contract?'

A little while after the race, Eddy Borysewicz – the famous Eddy B – who had coached Greg LeMond and Lance Armstrong and was now *directeur sportif* of the fledgling US Postal Service team, approached me. He said they needed a climber for the following season. We exchanged details and he left saying he'd be in touch. Before heading back to our hotel, I consoled a sobbing Jez Hunt, my teammate and a very talented sprinter who had failed to finish the race because the course simply didn't suit him. He too was close to turning pro and he thought he had blown his chance. I was convinced he'd turn pro and I told him it was only a matter of time.

That winter I waited for a call from US Postal Service that never came. My contact left the team without passing on my details. Meanwhile, Jez signed for Banesto, who had five-time Tour de France winner Miguel Indurain and were one of the biggest teams in the world.

I was devastated – not because Jez turned pro because he more than deserved it. It was just the way things worked out. Banesto, a team packed full of Spanish climbers, did not need someone like me, they needed a sprinter like Jez. I had just finished in the top ten in the World Championships, climbing with the best amateurs in the world, and I couldn't get a deal. What was I supposed to do?

* * *

I refused to give in. By now I was twenty-five going on twenty-six, an age when most people accept that their dreams are not going to come true and get on with real life.

I already had a proper job but I refused to push cycling to the fringes. I raced in Britain for another couple of years and felt I was continuing to improve. In 1998, I signed for the Harrods team.

Imagine that now, the world's most famous store sponsoring a cycling team. The reality was not quite as glamorous as it appeared. Mohamed Al-Fayed, the owner of Harrods, was not a cycling fan. Instead, the owner of the cycling franchise within the Knightsbridge store had persuaded Harrods to allow him to put their name to a cycling team. It turned out to be a good year, although I got some odd looks turning up for work at Marks and Spencer in Harrods cycling kit.

The best moment of my career came that year, on a Sunday afternoon in June in Solihull. With my whole family watching, I soloed to victory in the British national road race championship and had the honour of wearing the iconic white jersey with red and blue bands around the chest. I didn't sleep properly for days after that race and I'd wear the jersey round the house while drinking cups of tea. Every time I pulled on that jersey over the next twelve months gave me an immense sense of pride, which I still feel now. In fact, the jersey seems to have gained in prestige over the years. Whenever I've seen Geraint Thomas, Ian Stannard, Bradley Wiggins or Mark Cavendish in the national champion's jersey I think: 'I've got one of those hanging in my wardrobe.'

I stayed with the Harrods team for the 1999 season but the gold and green veneer was thin and was beginning to flake. The team folded midway through the year because the cycling franchise at Harrods was having financial difficulty. I wasn't without a team for long. The Linda McCartney squad threw me a lifeline. They'd actually tried to sign me at the start of the year but I stuck with Harrods. Now, they were offering me a place for the rest of the season and the possibility of a full professional contract for the 2000 season if I impressed them.

The *directeur sportif* was Sean Yates, who had graduated from the ACBB squad, had ridden for Peugeot and had worn the yellow jersey in the Tour de France – as well as the British national champion's jersey. He was also as hard as nails.

The Linda McCartney team had been founded in 1998 shortly before Linda died of cancer. The team was sponsored by the range of vegetarian Linda McCartney Foods and the idea was to promote a vegetarian diet and lifestyle. Sir Paul McCartney was also very supportive and although I didn't meet him, a lot of my teammates did. He even recorded a tune for the team's website.

The plan was to expand the team for the 2000 season and earn selection for one of the grand tours. This was my chance, perhaps my last chance. I was twenty-nine. This had to be it.

I rode well during the second half of 1999 and Sean told me the final place on the team for the following year was between me and a young British climber, Charly Wegelius. The Italian super team Mapei had their eyes on Charly so I hoped that would work out for him so I would get the final place at Linda McCartney.

My last big event of the year was the TransCanada

stage race. Charly was riding as a *stagiaire* – an amateur trialist – for McCartney. Later that autumn he
was offered a contract by Mapei, which opened the
door for me at McCartney.

I thought my chance had slipped away yet again
when I crashed heavily during the second stage,
breaking my collarbone and several ribs. The stem
that held my handlebars to the bike's frame had simply sheared off while I was riding at about forty miles
per hour. My injuries were so bad I couldn't travel
straight home, I had to stay with the team for the rest
of the time in Canada.

Then I spent two agonising weeks at home, recovering from the crash and waiting for the phone to
ring. When finally it came, I heard Sean's voice say,
with typical brevity and understatement 'You're in.'
He couldn't have known what those words meant to
me. More than fourteen years had passed since I'd
stood on Alpe d'Huez. The skinny kid who dreamed
of becoming a pro had finally made it. I was almost
thirty. I wasn't a dreamer, I knew my professional
career might not be a long one, but that didn't take
any of the shine off that moment.

* * *

I feel I had to explain the journey to put into context what it meant to be on the start line in Rome for

the 2000 Giro d'Italia. There had been near-misses all
along the way, but I had never been at all bitter. I was
not one of those 'I coulda been a contender' types. I
was confident I had the ability to be a professional
cyclist and I just wanted a chance.

The Linda McCartney team's profile had risen
with a number of high-profile recruits, notably Max
Sciandri, and we were the first British team to ride
one of the three grand tours since ANC-Halfords
tackled the Tour de France in 1987.

There was something quite appropriate about
the fact that the eighty-third Giro d'Italia started in
Rome, the Eternal City. Here I was, the thirty-year-
old new boy.

The day before the start, we'd been to the Vatican
for an audience with Pope John Paul II. It was all quite
unreal but I was prepared to savour every moment.
My seemingly interminable and unconventional path
to realising my childhood ambition had been realised.

*Here I was, at the Giro d'Italia. Matthew Stephens
alongside the modern greats of Italian cycling, Mario
Cipollini and Marco Pantani.*

One thing I had learned about the Giro d'Italia
was that it does not conform to any formula. The
Tour de France, particularly during the 1990s and
2000s, followed a well-worn pattern – a prologue followed by a week of flat stages, a long time trial to sort
the leading riders out, then the Alps and Pyrenees,

or the Pyrenees then Alps, with the mountain ranges linked by two or three lumpy transitional stages, then the flat run to Paris.

The Giro was a mixed bag right from the start. A look in the road book suggested there weren't any proper flat stages and we were due to hit the proper mountains as early as stage two. This gives the Giro an added layer of depth and makes for unpredictable and often extremely arduous racing.

Sprinkle into that some capriciously brutal weather and you have the ingredients to make the Giro the most revered and romanticised of the big tours.

* * *

The prologue in the Eternal City was held on a tight circuit with cobbled roads and ancient streets. My effort didn't see me light up the leaderboard but short time trials were never my strong point and I was just concentrating on finishing safely. I nearly came to grief on a nasty right-hander where someone's front door step jutted out into the road but I got round okay, in the lower quarter of the field but with one notable scalp. I had beaten the 1998 Giro and Tour winner Marco Pantani, not a rider known for his prowess in prologues, but no matter, I was off and running.

The opening road stage from Rome to Terracina was short by grand tour stages – only 125 kilometres

– and fast at the end but it was relatively straightforward and I finished in the bunch.

Stage two from Terracina to Maddaloni was when my grand tour dream turned dark. We started the 229-kilometre stage in thirty-degree sunshine and I'd decided to cover myself in sun cream before the start. I knew it was going to be a hard day – we were going to hit some difficult climbs.

Over the main climb of the day, I had managed to hold on to the lead group, which had whittled down to only fifty or so riders. I was feeling good up there in the front quarter of the field.

As we crossed the line for the king of the mountains prize at the top, the weather took a radical turn. The sky turned from a serene azure to a foul, malevolent grey. It started to rain. The smooth, shiny Tarmac became a skidpan. All the spilled diesel and accumulated dirt formed a greasy film on the surface of the road, which is treacherous for bicycle tyres. The rain was now a deluge, making it hard to see anything. The temperature plummeted too.

I watched as one rider after another fell. These are some of the best bike-handlers in the world but the conditions rendered their expertise almost useless.

Inevitably, my turn came on a gradual left-hander, a bend that we'd have taken at full speed in the dry, but which was now like an ice rink. My bike just went from under me and I hit the ground, along with two or three others. I jumped up in seconds, got back on my bike and rode on, the rain diluting the blood that was trickling from my elbow and knee.

I wove my way through the convoy of team cars following the main group – a move that is hazardous at the best of times. Eventually, squinting through the stinging rain, I could see the tail end of the group I'd been in.

One more effort and I could rejoin them, I thought. I sped through a small village and spotted a rider who had crashed, fifty metres in front. I was doing sixty kilometres an hour on this straight bit of road. I didn't need to do anything dramatic to avoid him. I just needed to steer gently round him. In the dry, this wouldn't have been anything out of the ordinary. It wasn't a violent or sudden move, just a subtle manoeuvre to give him room to pick himself up.

But in the wet my bike locked up and I began to aquaplane sideways. I probably looked like a cornering motorcycle speedway rider but without the same degree of control; in fact, without any degree of control. The bike was in charge, I was merely its terrified passenger.

My stomach tightened into a sickening clench. Every crash seems to happen in slow motion. There seem to be endless moments during which you are able to contemplate your fate before hitting the ground but this time I was agonisingly conscious of what was happening to me.

Suddenly my tyres regained purchase, gripping the road and throwing me sideways, off the bike. I hit the road with a revolting crunch.

The pain was immediate. It hurt, a lot. I lay in the road only briefly, then curled into a ball to protect myself from the cyclists and team cars swerving past me with their horns blaring.

I held my head but it was my knees that hurt the most. In a few moments a crowd had gathered round me and got me to the side of the road, out of danger of coming to further harm. It was chaotic. They were yelling and pointing at me. Before I knew it, some enthusiastic medics had me on a stretcher and were placing me in an ambulance.

No, no, this isn't in the script. I don't want to stop.

I tried to get off the stretcher but they weren't having it. I did the only thing I could to get the message across. I shouted in English with an Italian accent and gestured wildly that I wanted to get up. Eventually, they understood and I got off the stretcher and searched for my bike.

The race was still going past, so I still had a chance.

I got on my bike and realised I couldn't pedal. My knees were badly bashed and cut and they wouldn't go round without a fight.

By now the Linda McCartney team car was by my side. Sean wound the window down and I held on to the door with my left hand as we sailed through the flooded valley roads for a few kilometres to keep me in touch with the race while I assessed the damage. The freezing rainwater was splashing up to my ankles, I was wet through and my body temperature had plummeted, partly as a result of the weather, partly from the shock of the crash. It felt like I could feel my internal organs inside my shivering cavity. It was one of the strangest, scariest physical feelings I've ever had.

My legs were starting to lock up, so I used my right hand to push my right knee downwards, then pulled up by gripping the back of my knee with my fingers to fashion a sort of jerky pedalling action. After a few minutes doing this, I was able to pedal, although not with any power.

Incredibly, the rain got heavier. At points the road was more like a river with the water up to the hubs of my wheels and each pedal stroke giving my already sodden feet another dunking. I couldn't feel anything except the pain. My legs felt like they were made of railway sleepers, my knees rusty, ill-fitting hinges and my feet numb marshmallows.

I looked up and saw the banner said that there were fifty kilometres still to go. My heart sank, I felt like crying, but I rode on. My injuries meant I couldn't push hard enough to warm myself up. My teeth chattered, my hands lost feeling and I was unable to change gears. My team manager handed me a *bidon* – a water bottle – with hot, sweet coffee in it and that lifted my body temperature and my spirits just enough to keep going.

When I crossed the line in Maddaloni, last on the road, I was only just inside the time limit. I was twenty-five minutes behind the stage winner Cristian Moreni, almost eight minutes behind the next last group on the road. I'd been out there for six hours and forty minutes. I'd ridden the last couple of hours more or less on my own, all but convinced I was going to be eliminated.

When I crossed the line, the spectators had all gone home. They were starting to dismantle the Giro d'Italia. There was just me and a chap sweeping water away from the finish line with a broom, which was a pretty futile effort.

I don't know how I did it, but I do know why I did it.

I'd waited so long for this chance there was no way I was going to throw in the towel on the third day. We'd covered just over 350 kilometres and I didn't want to go home yet. I knew I might never get the opportunity to ride one of the great races again.

If you crash in a stage race, you get up and get to the finish if you possibly can. As long as you can pedal, you try to finish and then assess the injuries and see whether a good night's sleep can sort you out. If you abandon on the road, that's it, game over. If you cross the line inside the time limit, you have a stay of execution, so to speak.

Back at the hotel, I got patched up. Nothing was

broken and I didn't need stitches but I was covered in enough bandages I could have auditioned for a part in a Hammer House of Horror movie. I was covered in painful road rash. Both knees had taken a battering. I was struggling to walk, especially up and down stairs. I waddled, like a mummy. I wasn't sure I was going to be able to continue.

The following day was a 174-kilometre jaunt from Paestum to Scalea, as close to a routine flat stage as it was possible to get but, for me, a potential ordeal.

I rode from our hotel to the start to loosen my legs, which helped a little. But I found getting out of the saddle and putting all my body weight through my knees was problematic. I just hoped I could ride smartly, duck and dive a bit, shelter properly so I stayed out of the wind, and survive.

Before the start, a journalist from *La Gazzetta dello Sport* asked me a few questions about my antics with the ambulance the previous day, as well as the usual question about the team's vegetarianism and the now familiar: 'Have you met Sir Paul?'

Early in the stage Mario Cipollini, the Lion King himself, roared up alongside me and placed one hand on my shoulder. It was the cycling equivalent of being anointed by the Pope. Cipo was not only one of the most popular and charismatic sports people in Italy, he transcended sport. He had the air of a movie star. He was never far from his bodyguard, a super-fast

sports car or a line of beautiful women. He asked me
if I spoke Italian. I didn't, so we swapped a few words
in French. He said he'd been just behind me when
I crashed the second time and he thought I had no
chance of staying upright once my bike turned sideways. He then said he hadn't expected to see me at the
start today, considering how heavily I'd gone down.

Then he wished me luck and pedalled away, his
mane flowing and his oiled calves glistening, to sprinkle some star dust on someone else.

'What a very pleasant chap,' I thought.

I was not a star in the Giro d'Italia. I was one of
the extras needed to give the crowd scenes depth and
drama and to allow the stars to deliver their lines with
panache. Cipo didn't know me but he'd seen what had
happened and he sought me out to say a few words. It
was a moment that said much about the camaraderie in
the peloton and suggested too that Cipo's persona as a
brash, shallow showman was just on the exterior.

The next few stages were a challenging battle to
make it inside the time cut. For a few days I was the
maglia nera, figuratively at least. Between 1946 and
1951, the organisers presented a black jersey to the
last rider in the overall standings. Until stage 5 to
Peschici, I was that man.

The pain in my knees was getting worse but, oddly,
I felt strong otherwise. It sounds strange to say that
but I didn't feel weak, I just felt in pain. I couldn't

apply the force the rest of my body wanted to put down on the pedals. At the back of my mind I wondered if I was doing myself long-term damage but I decided that if I could finish inside the time cut I would not give up. I was driven on by the number of setbacks I'd had over the years. I felt I owed it to myself to carry on because I had believed in myself.

After the stage 11 time trial to Bibione, we had a rest day. Ever since the crash, I had been fixated on that rest day. My teammate David McKenzie even won a stage in between but that largely passed me by because I was engaged in my own personal battle.

I was looking forward to a chance to put my feet up and recuperate for a day after suffering for more than a week. In my mind, I had this picture of a little desert island of safety and tranquillity after being tossed around on the violently tempestuous ocean. I'd been clinging on to the raft, hoping not to get washed overboard, now I could relax a little.

But like all things that one looks forward to and enjoys, it was over all too quickly and I had that back to school feeling the night before the twelfth stage.

The pain of being on the bike was often unbearable. After that twelfth stage from Bibione to Feltre, I again spoke to our team doctor about the pain in both my knees. He went to see the race doctor who authorised and helped administer two steroid injections, one in each knee. I nearly panicked and refused the jabs when I saw the size of the cartoonishly large needle but the relief it gave me, if only for a few hours overnight, got me through the next two mountain stages virtually pain-free.

Stage 13 from Feltre to Selva Gardena climbed the fearsome Marmolada, via the Passo Fedaia. At one point, I was in a small group of six or seven riders, including Pantani. Riding on his wheel as the *tifosi* ran alongside him was surreal. He was like a god to them. At times it was frightening how close they got and how crazy they were. They were screaming in my ears and they were so close I could feel their breath on the side of my face. I was constantly worried about getting knocked off by a reckless fan, and even more concerned about bringing Pantani down with me. Riding in his company, although admittedly not at the front of the race – we were a fair way down on the leaders – coupled with the fact that the pain in my knees had subsided, allowing me to press properly on the pedals, gave me some much needed morale.

The fourteenth stage from Selva Gardena to Bormio, via the mythical, snow-lined Passo Gavia, was even more frightening. To make matters worse, I had slept badly and woke with a chesty cough.

The opening climb of the day was hard and I was one of the first to be dropped out of the back. For almost 100 kilometres I hung to the back of the race like a yo-yo. I was in touch for a while, then I'd fall back and would be in the convoy of team cars. Then I'd get up to them again and would hang in there for a bit before there was a change of gradient and I'd be dangling off the back again.

I was riding at my threshold but was struggling to breathe and my legs were screaming at me to stop. It was utter hell but I managed to get back to the bunch when they eased up as we approached the feed zone.

Once on the lower slopes of the Gavia, I settled into a sustainable rhythm and rode with a small group I knew I could stay with. In the last couple of kilometres, the weather changed. The air was thinner and each lungful burned. It was much colder and my breath was visible as I panted my way upwards.

Over the top, it was snowing so I put on my cape and grabbed a fistful of pink *Gazzetta* newspaper pages to shove down the front of my jersey – the old-fashioned way to stay warm on a freezing descent.

It didn't help much. Before long, I was frozen to the bone and the snow turned to sleet, making it dangerous. I was scared of crashing again and I could hardly brake because my hands were so cold.

Amazingly, the *directeur sportif* from the Amica Chips team handed me some thick gloves through the open window of his team car. He must have seen me and sympathised.

Because I was shaking and struggling to grip, I dropped one glove. There was no time to go back for it but I put the other one half on to my right hand, just enough to cover my fingers and enable me to use my front brake. My left hand was numb and useless. I made it down in one piece and made it to Bormio utterly spent. I wasn't last on the road, there were a few pour souls behind me, but I was just five minutes inside the time limit.

I nearly didn't start the fifteenth stage from Bormio to Brescia, a ride of 180 kilometres. My cough had worsened and the treatment for my knees had worn off. The race doctor would not authorise the contin-ued use of steroid injections because they were only masking the pain, not treating the underlying prob-lem. What I really needed was to rest. There were still seven stages until we reached Milan.

My teammates took turns to push me up the first climb of the day, which wasn't even ridden that hard. I clung on to the bunch until there were thirty kilo-metres to go. Then, I pulled the pin and let them go, knowing I would finish within the time cut.

* * *

That night, at the hotel, I spoke to the team doctor and to Sean Yates, my *directeur sportif,* and we decided I would not start the sixteenth stage the following morning. It hurt to pull the plug on my Giro but I was in danger of damaging my health. My knees weren't getting better, my cough was getting worse and I risked the rest of my season if I pushed on.

I cried, knowing that I wouldn't ride into Milan with the rest of the team.

My dream came to a close. I didn't get to ride the Giro d'Italia again, nor did I experience the Tour de France.

The crash defined my Giro. The conditions were harsh, sometimes barbaric. Long stages, terrible weather and a debilitating injury combined to ask me how far I was willing to push myself. In the aftermath of the crash I learned a lot about myself as a person, not just as a cyclist. I found my limit, tested just how much pain I could take, and discovered just what riding the Giro d'Italia, my only grand tour, meant to me.

Matt Stephens is a former professional road cyclist having ridden at World and Olympic level, who in 1998 became British National Road Race Champion. He spent thirteen years as a police officer with Cheshire Constabulary during a time that saw him blend law enforcement and racing as well as managing a domestic professional team. Following a few tentative forays into TV presenting on ITV's Tour of Britain and Tour Series coverage he plunged full time into 'talking 'bout cycling' and now is a regular commentator for Eurosport, a presenter for Global Cycling Network and a fledgling writer, having contributed pieces for Rouleur and now The Cycling Anthology. He lives in Bradford on Avon, collects old American superhero comic books and has no cats.

6

The Festina doping scandal threw the 1998 Tour de France and its Grand Départ in Dublin into turmoil.

Cycling was desperate for a saviour and the brilliance of Marco Pantani in the mountains appeared to be a gift sent from heaven.

As **Daniel Friebe** explains, Pantani's victory did not turn a fresh page for the sport.

This is the story of Italy's last great hurrah, a study of Pantani at his best and a look at the sudden descent that followed.

IL PIRATA

BY DANIEL FRIEBE

Conventional wisdom has it that Bradley Wiggins was the first Englishman to win the Tour de France, but conventional wisdom is wrong: the first Englishman to 'win' the Tour was Chris Boardman in 1998. If you don't believe it, sadly, Boardman won't either, and the man who wore the yellow jersey in Paris hasn't lived to tell the tale. Marco Pantani, you all know, died on Valentine's night in 2004.

But if he was still here, Pantani would tell you: Chris Boardman 'won' the 1998 Tour de France.

This is nothing to do with doping, nothing to do with a 2013 French Senate enquiry alleging that Pantani used EPO in the 1998 race (but which also, clearly, left him no right of reply). Amateur sleuths have already used that report as the basis for a revisionist rewrite of the 1998 Tour's general classification. Many have also hypothesised that Boardman was one of the small minority who didn't cede to temptation in the late 1990s, cycling's days of drug-fuelled decadence. But that's not what we're talking about here. And anyway, even if we were and even if he was clean,

Boardman's Tour did end with the Englishman in the yellow jersey – but three weeks early, after a crash on the second stage of the race.

It was that crash, during the stage from Enniscorthy to Cork in Ireland, that 'won' the Tour de France for Pantani.

One of *il Pirata's* teammates in that Tour, Mario Traversoni, remembers: 'Suddenly the wind started gusting really hard across the road. The other GC contenders and their teams knew that it was a great chance to attack Marco because he always rode at the back. I was our sprinter so I was the only one in the team with licence to ride near the front. The group shattered and I made the split, but Marco and the others were nowhere to be seen, and I started to fret. I dropped back to the second group, then the third, then the fourth, but still no sign. I reckon I ended up seeing fifteen little pockets of riders go past before, finally, this little yellow cloud appeared on the horizon with Marco in the middle. I then vividly remember the road turning left, the wind suddenly being in our face, and Boardman crashing up the road. The front group sat up, the pace died, and we were able to claw our way back. But that crash saved us. Without it, Marco would have lost five or six minutes and the Tour.'

That, you see, is how an Englishman 'won' the 1998 Tour de France.

* * *

This year marks the tenth anniversary of Marco Pantani's death. In May, a major tour returned to Ireland for the first time since the Tour de France in 1998. In a three-day *soggiorno*, the 2014 Giro d'Italia visited Belfast, skirted the Antrim coast and skimmed the Giant's Causeway before heading over the border to Dublin. The *Corsa Rosa* then journeyed home and climbed from the heel of Italy's boot to Trieste on the Slovenian border. On its way, the race paid homage to Pantani at Plan di Montecampione, where he administered the *coup de grâce* in his duel with Pavel Tonkov at the 1998 Giro, and the Santuario di Oropa, where he overtook fifty riders in the space of eight uphill kilometres to cause hysteria a year later.

Both in Dublin, where his triumphant 1998 Tour campaign started, and at Montecampione and Oropa, the air was thick with pathos and nostalgia. In a deeply moving piece written on the night of the climber's passing, *La Repubblica*'s Gianni Mura reflected glumly that, 'He'll probably become a myth, like they always do when they die young, or when we don't understand why they've gone.' And so it has proved. As Mura was fond of pointing out, Pantani won as many races in his entire career as Eddy Merckx typically used to manage in a season, yet the pair have spawned a similar number of books and monuments, and Pantani maybe even more shrill rhetoric.

In amongst all the eulogies and hand-wringing, however, a lot has also been forgotten. Like the fact that Pantani would never have won the Tour if Chris Boardman hadn't rammed into the back of his Gan teammate, Fred Moncassin, fifty-five kilometres from Cork. And that a Pantani victory seemed improbable, not to say impossible, long before he turned up in Ireland. The previous October, Pantani had fallen ill the night before he was due to attend the 1998 race presentation and cancelled his trip. When he glanced at the stage profiles the next day, he was relieved he hadn't bothered: 'Same old Tour de France,' he said, rolling his eyes at race director Jean-Marie Leblanc's latest ultra-conservative creation, with its mere two summit finishes. Pantani had already decided that he probably wouldn't even ride the 1998 Tour.

The likelihood of him appearing in Dublin didn't seem to improve with his victory in the Giro d'Italia in June. La Société du Tour de France had pushed the Grande Boucle back a week to avoid a clash with the football World Cup, but for much of June Pantani's energies were expended mainly on fishing trips or in the bars of the Riviera Romagnola, in his home town, Cesenatico or Rimini, where it would all end in a grubby hotel six years later. He raced once, at a criterium in Bologna on 8 June. A day or two later, he called his *directeur sportif* Giuseppe Martinelli: when he'd gone to get his bike out of the garage and it wasn't there, he remembered that he'd left it outside the showers in Bologna.

While Martinelli guided his Pantani clone Stefano Garzelli to victory in the Tour of Switzerland, *il Pirata* at least began to consider the possibility of riding in France. He summoned a group of teammates to Cesenatico and led the jamboree to familiar haunts: Monte Carpegna, Monte Fumaiolo, Le Balze or the roads sketching the circular route of the 'Giro delle Quattro Fontane' – the 'Tour of the Four Fountains', one of his favourite training routes. One day, at one of those fountains, Pantani turned to Roberto Conti, his mountain sherpa.

'If I go to the Tour, what do you think I can do?' he wondered aloud.

'Well,' Conti said, 'it'll be hard to beat Ullrich, with two time trials, but behind him it's anyone's . . .

Pantani paused for a moment then delivered his response with a smirk that encouraged rather than allayed doubts: 'Well if you say that, I reckon I can win it. Let's go then . . .'

In his mind, Pantani was still hesitating, but then something happened to force his choice: Luciano Pezzi, the former rider who had become Pantani's confidant and persuaded the Mercatone Uno supermarket chain to build a team around him in 1997, died, aged seventy-seven, on 26 June. The next day, as they and the other mourners shuffled out of the cemetery in Dozza, Pantani pulled Martinelli aside. 'I'm going to France. I'm going to ride the Tour,' he whispered. It would be his farewell gift to Pezzi, the first and until then perhaps the only man to really believe that he could do the Giro–Tour double.

Pantani thus arrived in Dublin with just over a fortnight's training in his legs. He was in a relaxed mood, although not overly enamoured with Ireland. 'To me, the Tour should start in France just like the Giro should start in Italy,' he mumbled as the plane swooped in to land. News was about to break that the Festina *soigneur*, Willy Voet, had been arrested with a vast cargo of doping products at the Belgian border. The next day, though, even as that scandal began to escalate and panic spread through hotel corridors, Pantani was all smiles at the team presentation. He waved to the crowd then giggled when his former Carrera teammate, Stephen Roche, playfully yanked a baseball cap over his eyes.

It was almost tempting in those first few days to think that Pantani wasn't taking the Tour very seriously. When riders were finally allowed to train on the prologue course on the morning of the *Grand Départ*, Pantani stayed in his room. He later doddered around the 5.6-kilometre course forty-eight seconds slower than Boardman and forty-three behind Ullrich to finish 181st out of 188 riders. He lacked racing rhythm but possibly lost more time as a result of not having a clue where the road was going. Martinelli tried dictating corner-by-corner instructions into his ear-piece – 'Left here, right in 100 metres . . .' – but Pantani continued to stray wildly from the recommended lines.

It was a neat encapsulation of Pantani and his relationship with Martinelli. 'Martino', a former pro from Brescia with a thin smile and raspy north-ern accent, had quickly learned when Pantani joined Carrera that managing him required the deftness of a bomb disposal expert and the intuition of a chess grandmaster. Where the other star at Carrera, Claudio Chiappucci, carried himself with brash, luminous confidence, Pantani's anxieties never lurked far below the surface. Given their differences and their simi-lar skills as riders, it was almost inevitable that they couldn't cohabit for long. One former teammate, Nicola Miceli, claims there was a furious argument between the team manager, Davide Boifava, and what Miceli calls 'a notorious coach' – almost certainly Francesco Conconi – at the end of Pantani's break-through 1994 season: Conconi had made Pantani too good, too quickly (according to computer files seized by police, Conconi had 'boosted' Pantani's haemat-ocrit from 40.7 per cent on 16 March to 57.4 per cent by the end of the 1994 Tour de France) and now he was demanding a pay rise that stretched the team's budget. Chiappucci and Pantani finally went their

separate ways – Chiappucci to Asics and an ignominious swansong, Pantani to Mercatone Uno and
superstardom in 1997.

Pantani had wanted Martinelli at Mercatone Uno
because he was one of the rare team directors who tol-
erated the kind of tactics that Pantani would employ
in the first week of the 1998 Tour. Joining Mercatone
Uno had given him the guarantee of unreserved team
support and the authority to impose his unorthodox
technique of riding at the very tail end of the peloton,
in a cocoon of *domestiques*. Over the years, a consen-
sus had built among cycling sages that this equated
to hara-kiri at the Tour de France, where the peloton became a moving minefield and a crash or split
could detonate the chances of anyone stranded on the
wrong side. Pantani didn't care. It had always looked
to him as though the stress of staying at the front and
the risk of languishing at the back were more or less
an even trade. If he did find himself cut adrift, his
teammates would just have to adopt team time trial
formation and haul him back to safety. At least this
way he always knew where they were. Former teammates now say that, in retrospect, Pantani's habit of
constantly looking over his shoulder to check their
position was one of the earliest, plainest outward signs
of the insecurities that later tore him apart.

At the 1998 Tour, until the mountains, a com-
forting haze of pale yellow Mercatone Uno jerseys

would fill Pantani's sightline. His only concession, a
kind of added insurance policy, was allowing Mario
Traversoni to contest bunch sprints in the hope of
picking up bonus seconds and moving up the GC.
With the position of team cars in the race convoy
dictated by their best rider's overall position, this was
the only way to get Martinelli closer to Pantani and
his yellow bubble. The theory was good, the execution less so: Traversoni never made it into the top 100
overall and by the third day had thrown a strop about
the pointlessness of bringing a sprinter to the Tour
and not supporting him.

The other members of the Mercatone Uno clan
insist today that they had rarely seen Pantani so
serene. Marco Velo, who wasn't at the Tour but would
become a key disciple in later years, says that serving
Pantani 'was like studying for a degree in psychology'.
He could be prickly, needy and yet at the same time
unapproachable, particularly at major tours. Here,
though, he looked like he was on a summer jaunt. The
spiralling Festina scandal and the prospect of something bigger engulfing the whole peloton appeared
to cause him no concern, or at least none that
colleagues at Mercatone Uno have since admitted. We
know now that, for peace of mind, other riders and
teams had dispensed with their drugs either in Ireland
or by the time that Festina were finally kicked out
of the race on 18 July. But apparently not Pantani:

by cross-referencing documents compiled in the 2013 French Senate report into doping, we can see that Pantani's urine samples were heavily contaminated with EPO after stages 11, 15 and 16. Given what we know about EPO detection windows, it therefore seems highly likely that he injected EPO at regular intervals throughout the Tour.

There was certainly no doubt that his legs were starting to purr as the Tour forged on down the western half of France. Leblanc's dour, multi-course menu of relentlessly flat stages in the first week was expected to cause Pantani some indigestion – and at times he had been hanging on. But to be only five minutes behind the new race leader, Jan Ullrich, after a hot, gnarly fifty-eight-kilometre time trial in Limousin on the first Saturday felt like a triumph. Festina and their lachrymose leader Richard Virenque were finally expelled on the same day. Pantani wasn't fazed; not only had he never liked or rated the Frenchman, but in his own way he was getting into the zone, the same psychological sweet spot that he'd found at the Giro in June. Asked about Festina, he responded coolly and in terms that with hindsight stunk of hypocrisy but also a sense of entrapment shared by a lot of his contemporaries: 'The police and the justice system need to take care of it, and CONI (the Italian Olympic Committee) needs to get its act together: they need to finally develop detection methods for the products that don't show up in tests.' And on the race, he had lapsed into the excessively cagey, almost gleefully self-deprecating mode that Martinelli had come to recognise as the harbinger of big things: 'I couldn't go too hard [in the time trial], otherwise I'd have paid for it over the next few days. I'm not in good condition. From this point there's a big question mark over my head.'

Privately, though, there were clear hints that his confidence was growing as the Pyrenees approached. One night, Luciano Pezzi's son Fausto visited the team hotel and bumped into Pantani in the lift. 'I'm sorry about your dad,' Pantani told him. 'You must miss his words, because I do. We can't just go through the motions here now . . .'

And the night before stage 8 to Montauban, he went for a stroll in the hotel garden with his *domestique* and fellow *romagnolo,* Fabio Fontanelli. Fontanelli was having a wretched Tour and thinking of abandoning. 'You stay here, because we're going to have some fun,' Pantani told him in their local dialect.

On the eve of the race, Gianni Mura, the only man in the Tour de France press room who still used a typewriter, had punched these prophetic words into his Olivetti Lettera 32: 'Marco Pantani's Tour starts on 21 July.'

It was the date of stage 10, when the Tour would brave the infamous *'Cercle de la Mort'* or 'Ring of

Death' – the passes of the Aubisque, Tourmalet, Aspin
and Peyresourde – en route to Luchon.

Pantani was ready. The games could begin.

* * *

The shift in momentum from Jan Ullrich to Marco
Pantani in back-to-back Pyrenean stages could be dis-
cerned from the facial expressions of their respective
directeurs sportifs. When Pantani skipped away from
the German two kilometres from the summit of the
Peyresourde – in cold, misty conditions that recalled
his win at nearby Guzet Neige three years earlier –
Martinelli's eyes sparkled in the gloom. The next day,
the same thing happened when, having punctured at
the foot of the final climb to Plateau de Beille, Ullrich
sprinted past Martinelli's wound-down window, his
lungs throbbing like bagpipes. A second or two later,
Martinelli heard the growl of an engine and glanced
across at his counterpart, Rudy Pevenage, huffing and
puffing behind the wheel of his team Telekom Audi. In
his wing mirror, Martinelli could see a confetti of pink
and white Telekom jerseys. As he would again later
in the Tour, Ullrich had shattered himself and blown
away his teammates by trying to recover too quickly.

In Luchon, Pantani hadn't caught his compatriot
Rodolfo Massi but did finish second and gained twenty-three seconds on Ullrich. The following morning,

on the drive from their hotel in Spain, Pantani frowned at the route profile showing in the roadbook open on Martinelli's dashboard. 'I thought it was a summit finish today . . .' he said, turning to his *directeur*.

Martinelli again smiled: the book was open at the wrong page. For a rider who could easily get mired in his own thoughts and fears – or what he idiosyncratically called 'mental masturbations' – Pantani had been positively Zen-like since the start of the Tour.

That afternoon, low down on the long, gruelling climb to Plateau de Beille, Pantani had begun the ritual striptease that was now the prelude to all of his attacks in the mountains, first peeling off his sunglasses then his bandana. He went to accelerate but felt a tug on his jersey. It was Roberto Conti pulling him back. 'Oi! Ullrich's punctured, you can't attack now . . .' Pantani hadn't seen him. He now sunk back into his saddle, waited for Ullrich's yellow jersey to appear over his shoulder, gave the German just over two minutes to catch his breath, then bulleted off down the road. This time he was irresistible. He crossed the line one minute and forty seconds before Ullrich.

Pantani was now up to fourth on general classification, three minutes adrift of the 1997 winner. If he didn't fully believe before, he did now: he spent the evening making sure that, from this point on, he'd know exactly what was coming next, poring over route profiles in his room.

In the start village the next morning, Roberto Conti felt a tap on his shoulder. It was one of Ullrich's *domestiques* – Conti can't remember which one. 'Eh,' he said, 'I see what you're doing: taking two minutes here, two minutes there, getting closer and closer but never helping us out . . .'

Conti did his best to look bashful. 'No,' he said. 'We're just here for stage wins. We're not interested in winning the Tour.'

Which was a bare-faced lie.

* * *

Of all of the adjectives commonly used to describe Pantani, 'unpredictable' is probably the one that fits worst. Because while his attacks would frequently defy logic, they were rarely a surprise. In fact, as *La Gazzetta dello Sport* journalist Marco Pastonesi would point out after another Pantani masterpiece at Oropa at the 1999 Giro, one of the climber's unique talents was the ability to reliably – predictably – deliver what seemed extraordinary. 'Pantani's every acceleration is a little treasure, which no one needs to keep secret; it's money in the bank, in the bank of our senses and our memory, free money,' Pastonesi wrote.

Another journalist, Gianni Mura, had also seen enough cycling in his thirty-three years following the Giro and the Tour to know that the only things certain in life were death, taxes and Pantani attacking in the mountains. At Plateau de Beille, speaking to Mura, Pantani had uttered his most memorable sound bite, an aphorism to sit alongside the victories that would make up his legacy: '*In salita vado forte solo per abbreviare la mia agonia*' – 'I only climb so fast to abbreviate my agony'. Mura thought that Pantani spoke more like a poet than a cyclist. But then, Mura had fallen under his spell. The reality was that Pantani's monologues could be long, meandering and peppered with clichés. Very occasionally, it's true, his turns of phrase might sound unusually abstract and even recherché, but Mura's claim that 'the fascination of Pantani was that of an undiscovered island or continent' proves that *il Pirata*'s talent for climbing mountains had perhaps already been surpassed by his gift for creating mystique.

In the press room in Grenoble on 26 July, the night before the Alpine death-match over the Galibier, Mura stubbed out his last cigarette of the afternoon and lifted the script from his teal-green Lettera 32 machine. In his accustomed, weary manner, the old walrus then picked up a telephone and dialled the number of *La Repubblica*'s copy desk in Rome. Spelling out the words in the usual Italian way – where every letter was the initial of a city, and so 'Pantani' became 'Palermo, Ancona, Napoli, Torino, Ancona, Napoli, Imola', like stages of a Giro too flat for *il Pirata*'s palate – Mura filed another of his prescient dispatches. In it, he related a conversation that he'd had earlier that day with Alfredo Martini, a sort of pontiff of Italian cycling and winner of six rainbow jerseys as the Italian national coach between 1975 and 1997. Martini had told Mura – and so Mura had written – that Pantani should attack on the steep hairpins just beyond Plan Lachat, six kilometres from the summit of the Galibier.

The next afternoon, six kilometres from the top of the Galibier, away Pantani went into the freezing fog.

What happened next is now part of Tour folklore, indeed one of its most fabled chapters: Pantani crested the 2,645-metre Galibier summit three minutes and ten seconds ahead of Ullrich and was by then *maillot jaune virtuel.* Forty-two kilometres later, he had crossed the line at Les Deux Alpes a staggering eight minutes and 57 seconds ahead of Ullrich. He now led the Tour by almost four minutes from the American Bobby Julich and by nearly six from Ullrich, the 'future five-time Tour winner' hailed only a year earlier by Bernard Hinault.

Ullrich had already looked close to capitulation a kilometre from the top of the Galibier. He then repeated the error that he'd made at Plateau de Beille, panicking after a puncture at the foot of the climb to Les Deux Alpes and exhausting himself in pursuit of Julich. At the finish, his previously chiselled features were bloated beyond recognition – some speculated as a result of cortisone use. What we can now deduce from the 2013 French Senate report is that Pantani and Ullrich were doped with EPO and would take more of the drug before the end of the race. Julich had been confronted by his wife about the Festina revelations during the first week and confessed to her that he had been cheating with EPO since 1996. The American claims to have taken his last-ever dose at some point during the Tour, but hasn't said exactly when. It's also not clear from French Senate records whether Julich, like Pantani and Ullrich, was doped on EPO in the Alps. Julich didn't respond to a request for clarification in February 2014.

As far as Pantani was concerned, it wasn't EPO or even his legs that had propelled him through the deluge, but mental strength. 'I think I had the strongest head of all today,' he said. The front page of *L'Équipe* the next morning would show the moment of Pantani's attack under the headline: *C'EST UN GÉANT* – HE'S A GIANT.

His teammates had seen him for the last time at the foot of the Galibier. Pantani had clipped a wheel, fallen on to a rock, then wiped himself down while they checked his bike. He had then hopped back on and sped off up the road, *à la* Ullrich, only without over-revving his engine like the German. When Mario Traversoni lurched under the king of the mountains banner an hour or so later, the third Mercatone Uno *directeur sportif* Orlando Maini was already star-jumping in celebration at the side of road and bawling the good news that Pantani was riding into yellow. Unfortunately, in his excitement, Maini forgot that he had a job to do; the rain cape that he was supposed to pass to Traversoni was still fluttering in his hand when the sprinter disappeared over the brow and down the descent, shivering and appalled.

* * *

In the six stages that remained of the 1998 Tour de France, the biggest threat to Pantani would come not from Ullrich, not from what was left of the Alps but the possibility of the race not reaching the Champs-Élysées.

Twenty-four hours after his Galibier knockdown, Ullrich had hauled himself off the canvas and come out swinging on the Col de la Madeleine, but Pantani matched him blow for blow. He even resisted the urge to drop his rival on the climb, then squeezed his brake-levers on the finishing straight in Albertville to present Ullrich with the stage win. It was the done thing and also the smart one; as another Italian Niccolò Machiavelli once advised, it's best to keep your friends close and your enemies closer.

Pantani was much more at home practising this kind of diplomacy than the politics required in his new, de facto role as 'patron of the peloton'. With more police raids came more complaints from the riders and more schisms between them. Stage 17 was a new nadir. For an hour or two, the race looked in danger of stopping altogether until negotiations between race director Jean-Marie Leblanc, the French sports minister and the riders' various factions ended in an uneasy truce: they would hold a go-slow – an '*opération escargot*', as the French call it – before ripping off their race numbers just before the finish in Aix-Les-Bains, rendering the stage null and void. Six entire teams had decided that enough was enough and wouldn't start stage 18 the following day. The manager of the Spanish ONCE outfit, Manolo Saiz, had gone out with a flourish, or more precisely the parting message: 'I have stuck my finger up the Tour de France's arse.'

Newspapers juxtaposed scathing coverage of Saiz and his fellow deserters with their praise for Pantani, who was in the process, they said, of 'saving the Tour de France'. While early in the race French newspaper *Libération* had decried a 'cesspit' of a sport, suggesting that 'the giants of the road are dwarves of sporting morality', a more common view was that all of the bad apples had been jettisoned; the 1998 Tour might therefore be one of the cleanest of all time. Alas, a fifteen-year drip feed of uncomfortable truths, culminating in the 2013 Senate report, has dispelled that idea.

On the road, Pantani still needed to defend a lead of more than five-and-a-half minutes over both Julich and Ullrich in the final time trial to Le Creusot. He did it comfortably, despite Ullrich claiming a consolatory stage victory. At the Giro, his teammates and even Martinelli had shaved their heads in Pantani's honour on the last day. Now they dyed their hair yellow, like Marco's sister Manola back in Cesenatico. Pantani dyed his goatee beard.

On the Champs-Élysées, Pantani's arm was held aloft by the last Italian to win the Grande Boucle, 1965 champion Felice Gimondi. Pantani surprised himself: he had mentally prepared for the moment, and didn't expect to get emotional, but was shocked to feel himself welling up. Mainly, though, he was tired. So tired, in fact, that he didn't even partake in another end-of-Tour tradition – the night out in Paris – and instead got on a plane straight back to Italy.

***

The immediate postscript to the story ended with Pantani's last competitive outing of 1998 and an incongruous sprint-win over Ullrich in a criterium in Luxembourg on 21 September. A much broader and more sombre narrative, of course, continued through to his death in 2004 and is still unfolding today. As much a commemoration of Pantani's life and achievements, and an invitation to reflect on who and what had caused a national sporting tragedy, Valentine's Day 2014 demonstrated once again how Italy's love affair with cycling had ended with Pantani. A decade on, his is still the only name that truly resonates with the casual fan. 'It's like the sport has fallen into post-traumatic stress and never been able to wake up,' says Filippo Pozzato, one of the generation that came immediately after Pantani. Pozzato disputes the idea, now finally popular after years of denial, that professional cycling in Italy is on life support: 'It's not nearly dead. It *is* dead,' he says.

It would be disingenuous, though, to say that whatever malaise has taken hold stems solely from Pantani. To chart the slow decline of the sport in Italy since the millennium is also to chronicle the recent history of a nation in decay. If there are only two elite Italian cycling teams in 2014, it is as much due to the weakness of the economy as it is to Pantani, his peers and how their doping sapped the public's faith and enthusiasm. It is also about natural change, societal evolution, and not just avoidable self-harm; professional cycling was popular in Italy before the Second World War, and became even more so on the coat-tails of what became known as the Italian Economic Miracle, Italy's industrial growth spurt, in the 1950s and 60s. Cycling fans were the same men and women – mainly men – who had brought Italy new wealth with their hard graft in the factories and fields, and who identified with the toil of working-class heroes seeking fame aboard their bikes. This symbiosis lasted, particularly in the northern regions, for as long as Italy's manufacturing base was still thriving – namely until around the time when Pantani began his precipitous fall. In 1995, if we take GDP as our measure, Italy was the fifth richest nation in the world. In 2013, it wasn't even in the top ten.

As John Foot, a professor of Italian at Bristol University and the author of *Pedalare! Pedalare!* puts it: 'Pantani's heyday coincided with the last time that Italy really held its head high as a nation. The political system was falling apart in the 1990s, with the *Tangentopoli* scandal (literally "Bribesville"), and Berlusconi had started his first term in office in 1994, but it all started to really collapse when the Euro was introduced in 1999. That marked a kind of watershed. And now, well, Italy has become a bit of a joke, to its own people even more than internationally. Pantani was something, someone that Italians were proud of. Now they're not proud of very much at all.'

Thus, Italians perhaps hold on to Pantani and his memory as a souvenir of better days. Or if not better, then at least very different ones. 'The Italy that fell in love with Pantani was an Italy that loved all the rhetoric about sacrifice and suffering that cycling was supposedly all about,' says Foot. 'Young Italians now find nothing attractive in that. They're much more interested in glamour, speed, those things. Consequently, for them, the MotoGP pilot who died [in 2011], Marco Simoncelli, is much more of a cult figure than Pantani.'

Filippo Pozzato agrees: 'Cycling is made to look sexy with the way it's presented and marketed in countries like the UK. In Italy it's not sexy at all. It's all grainy black and white film of Fausto Coppi, endless droning on about how tough it is. No wonder kids aren't interested.'

In some ways, then, the martyr could have been anyone. But of course that's not true, either. Pantani was uniquely placed to become Italian cycling's pied piper for many reasons. A frail, sylph-like figure who had started to lose his hair when he was fourteen, he was a perfect protagonist in an underdog story even before all of those crashes early in his career. He was thrilling, beautiful and brave on the bike, but also rode it with a certain nonchalance, what the Italians in the Renaissance called '*sprezzatura*'. When discussing his training, he quoted not heart rates and wattages, but names of places, mountains, regions that the average Italian could find on a map or had visited on holiday in their camper vans. He refused to even time himself on climbs, explaining, 'I like to listen to what my body and the mountain are telling me, nothing else.' On rides, rather than new-fangled energy bars or gels, he ate a handful of hazelnuts or a slice of watermelon, and drunk so little that his teammate Fabio Fontanelli had

christened him 'The Camel'. The same 'prehistoric' ten-
dencies had earned him another nickname, 'The Fossil',
from Gianni Mura. Whatever you called the winning
mix, Pantani had enough in common with the ordinary
Italian to make him seem familiar, while also retaining
an enigmatic side that stirred the imagination.

He was also adept at perpetuating an illusion: his
mid-race snacks may not have been hi-tech, but his
'medical preparation' certainly was. But, again, these
were different times, the final days of widespread
naivety; Pantani's 1998 Giro win, and to a lesser
extent also his Tour victory two months later, were
the very last major tours in which remarkable physical
feats invoked swoons before suspicion.

If those few lines are a crude summation of what
makes Pantani so hard for Italy to forget, there is
little point in ending on a beermat breakdown of why
he died – not when people have been producing and
arguing over the reasons for years. Suffice it to say that
there are many like his old Carrera teammate and
friend Nicola Miceli, who says that he is haunted by
one regret – 'That I didn't go down there to Cesenatico
to talk to him, tell him that I'd been depressed for
three years when I had to stop racing, tell him that it
was normal and that he had to reinvent himself . . .';
many like Marco Velo, his *ex-gregario*, who has concluded that Pantani's personality was, like the drugs
that ended up killing him, a deadly cocktail – 'great

vulnerability, a constant need for reassurance, yet at the same time a grave distrust and unwillingness to listen . . .'; and even those like Mattia Gavazzi, a professional cyclist who has fought cocaine addiction and can't quite bring himself to feel sorry for Pantani, 'because ultimately I've realised that you have to pull yourself out of it, with the help of other people but mainly with your own determination.'

As for wise old Gianni Mura, well, after the one about Pantani's 1998 Tour starting on 21 July and the one about the Galibier, he really had made a third accurate prediction with that piece filed late – as he said 'too late, too late for so many things' – on the night of 14 February 2004: 'He'll probably become a myth, like they always do when they die young, or when we don't understand why they've gone . . .'

After which Mura had hesitated over the keys of his faithful Olivetti, then added his bitter final line:

'I would rather have watched him grow old, and gone for a glass of Sangiovese with him, somewhere up there in his hills.'

Daniel Friebe has covered every Tour de France since 2001, when he still comfortably qualified for the white jersey. Now *Procycling*'s European Editor, he is the author of *Eddy Merckx: The Cannibal, Mountain High* and its sequel *Mountain Higher,* and collaborated with Mark Cavendish on his best-selling autobiographies, *Boy Racer* and *At Speed.*

7

Keith Bingham was there when the Tour de France first visited England in 1974.

He watched them arrive by plane, stood by the roadside and observed these exotic Continental creatures during their flying visit to Devon, who British cycling fans had until then only read about.

He explains why the Tour came across the English channel for a stage anyway, wonders why it took 20 years to come back again and remembers the sheer magic and majesty of seeing Eddy Merckx and the greatest riders in the world on British roads.

A DAY TRIP TO DEVON

BY KEITH BINGHAM

When the Tour de France visited the south coast of England for two days in 1994, the yellow jersey was worn on either side of the channel by two British riders, Chris Boardman and Sean Yates. When London hosted the Grand Départ in 2007, five British riders were on the start line, the largest contingent for twenty years. In 2014, as Leeds became the most northerly city to host the start of the Tour, it could be argued that British cycling ruled the world, after back-to-back victories for Bradley Wiggins and Chris Froome and with Mark Cavendish closing in on Eddy Merckx's record tally of stage victories.

But the Tour's first sojourn to England was in 1974 when Barry Hoban, with six stage wins to his name at that point, was the closest thing British cycling had to Mark Cavendish.

The 1974 Tour started with a prologue in Brest in Brittany, before an opening road stage to Saint-Pol-de-Léon, not far from Roscoff on the north Breton coast. Then the race went overseas for the first time – there had been frequent excursions outside France, into Belgium, Holland, Switzerland and Spain but this was the first time the Tour would cross water to seek new ground.

Stage 2 was held in Plymouth, Devon, or to be more precise on a circuit that went up and down the recently opened A38 Plympton bypass.

Although it was estimated that only 15,000 spectators watched the race, as opposed to the hundreds of thousands, possibly millions, who have lined the roads on subsequent visits to England, the event was deemed a success.

In the 1960s and 1970s, cycling was the Cinderella of sports in Britain. It was an oddity, but not one that piqued the interest of the masses. But for me, a rookie cycling reporter who had yet to cover the Continental scene that seemed so vivid, so glamorous and yet so distant, and for the small but dedicated band of cycling fanatics, the day the Tour came to Devon is etched in the mind.

Today, with hours of live television coverage of not just the Tour de France, the Giro d'Italia and the Classics, but also smaller races, it's hard to imagine what it was like back then. Our craving could only be partially satisfied by the reports and photographs in cycling magazines. In the 1950s, which was before my time, Fausto Coppi had entered the Manx Premier pro race on the Isle of Man and Coppi and Jacques Anquetil had raced in a famous track meeting at the

Herne Hill velodrome in south-east London. But even when Tom Simpson won the professional road race at the World Championships in 1965, we saw only a few seconds of film of him crossing the line on the news. We expected a major breakthrough when Simpson won the BBC's Sports Personality of the Year award but it never came. Cycling never quite caught on with the British public.

Simpson's death on Mont Ventoux during the 1967 Tour put cycling on the front pages and the horrific footage of Simpson weaving from side to side and then coming to a standstill before falling from his bike drove me to tears.

After that, the public understood the severity of the Tour and, perhaps, respected that it had the power to push men beyond their limits. It gained a reputation as the toughest endurance contest on the planet but still it did not win people over. The Tour was a killer.

Even when Graham Webb and Beryl Burton won the men's and women's amateur road race titles on the same day at the World Championships in Heerlen, the Netherlands, later that same year, cycling struggled to break out from the bottom corner of a tucked-away page in the sports section.

When Burton returned home to Yorkshire with her world champion's rainbow jersey, very few people gave her or her bike a second glance as she stepped off the train at Leeds.

To illustrate British indifference, I can recall a television news feature that completely misunderstood the point of the Tour and its following *caravane publicitaire* by portraying it not as the hardest sporting marathon in the world but as a big travelling circus, a jolly cycle trip round France in the company of acrobats and advertising floats. The film showed the riders freewheeling along, reaching out to take hats from spectators and horsing about. Undoubtedly this had happened during downtime in the daily stages but it gave the impression that the Tour was a travelling roadshow. Clearly the film crew had only bothered to film the opening kilometres of a stage, when the race was still neutralised as it made its way out of town, before the hard work began.

I remember feeling so annoyed at this wasted opportunity to show the true nature of the Tour: the drama, the rivalries, the grit and toughness.

There were, of course, hardy and determined enthusiasts who would travel over to the Continent, often by bicycle, to watch the big events, but for most of us the first opportunity to see these exotic racing creatures in the flesh was when the World Championships were held in Leicester in 1970. I felt a sense of disappointment at seeing the star riders in their national team colours instead of in their trade team colours. We'd see only the occasional colour photograph of the Molteni, Bic, Sonolor, Gan-Mercier,

Peugeot-Michelin and Brooklyn jerseys that made up the evocative Continental peloton.

Some enthusiasts wondered whether the Tour would lose some of its French charm as it headed across the channel and when it was announced that the Devon stage would be a simple circuit race on the Plympton bypass, with the riders going up one side of the dual carriageway and down the other, those fears seemed to be confirmed.

We assumed that the authorities wanted to avoid closing roads across a wider area of the county and didn't find out until much later that it was the Tour de France organisers who wanted the race contained in a smaller area to make the logistical exercise simpler. Alf Palmer, who was charged with organising the Devon stage, said he had permission to head out into Dartmoor but the Tour organisers wanted to make sure they could get back to France quickly as soon as the race was over.

But it didn't matter. The Tour de France coming to England was an exciting prospect. We didn't care that the best cyclists in the world would be completing laps of a rather uninspiring circuit on a near-deserted dual carriageway. We focused on the fact that the fourteen-lap race would mean we'd get to see the stars twenty-eight times. We would be going to Plymouth come hell or high water.

* * *

ALF PALMER: THE MAN WHO BROUGHT
THE TOUR TO BRITAIN

In 1994, southern England hosted two stages, one
from Dover to Brighton, the other started and finished in Portsmouth, looping into the Hampshire
countryside. The Tour's visit then was to commem-
orate the fiftieth anniversary of the D-Day landings
and to mark the opening of the channel tunnel.

The Tour's visit to Plymouth twenty years earlier
had been a purely commercial venture, designed to
promote trade links between Devon and Brittany and
publicise the new Roscoff to Plymouth ferry link,
which carried the region's produce, including artichokes, from northern France to Britain.

The main instigator of this historic event was the
Brittany Economic Committee, recalls Alf Palmer,
who was appointed director of the Tour's organising
committee by Plymouth District Council.

Palmer, then aged thirty-eight, was the secretary to
Plymouth's Lord Mayor and, fittingly, was responsible
for all ceremonial occasions. He was a cyclist and a
member of the Plymouth club, St Budeaux CC, and
organised the club's annual twenty-five-mile time trial.

It was quite a jump to go from organising a club
'25' to putting on a stage of the world's biggest bike
race but Palmer's background in cycling meant he was
the obvious man to take on the task.

'It was a case that when the situation arose that the Tour was coming to Plymouth, it fell to them [the district council] to arrange things, and the town clerk didn't know anything about cycling,' he says. 'Someone in the office told them that I was a cyclist and so they asked if I would be interested in doing it.'

Orchestrating the Tour's first visit to these shores took an enormous amount of work and research, perhaps more so than today because there was not the understanding of the event we now have.

Palmer looks back proudly at how Plymouth played its part in creating sporting history and so it is with a sense of annoyance that the Tour's first visit was overlooked when, two decades later, the Tour returned to southern England.

'I do get the feeling sometimes that the cycling world rather wishes the Plymouth stage had not taken place and that the 1994 visit represented the first visit to these shores,' he says. 'It should not be forgotten that in 1974 the complete closing of roads for a cycle race was a unique event. By the time 1994 came around, attitudes had changed completely.'

Palmer corrects the mistaken view that the new Plympton bypass was only chosen for the 1974 stage because it had not yet been opened to the public. In fact, the road had been opened some months before.

'It was not an "unopened stretch of highway", as people say, but it had been operational for several months,' he says. 'Although it is now the main trunk road link between Devon and Cornwall, at the time it was probably felt that its closure for the day would not be of enormous inconvenience to traffic bypassing Plymouth because it was comparatively new and people were still familiar with the roads they had used before it was opened.'

However, there was still a lot of negotiating to do before the authorities confirmed the road closure and the Tour's organisers were required to be out of the way so the road could be reopened within half an hour of the stage finishing.

Over the years, people have wondered why, when the Tour had gone to all the logistical effort of crossing the channel, the stage was held on a bland bypass rather than taking a trip into the beautiful Devon countryside. The organising committee, which included the organiser of the Milk Race, Phil Liggett, as technical advisor, wanted to take the Tour into Dartmoor and proposed two stunning routes.

At the time, many assumed it was because it suited the Department of Transport but actually it was because it suited the Tour de France organisers.

'The reason I feel the bypass was chosen was predominantly to facilitate the ease of the riders and the Tour entourage so they could access Exeter airport and the Plymouth ferry port,' says Palmer.

Together with his team, Palmer travelled to the

office in Paris that the Tour organisers shared with the sports paper *L'Équipe* to discuss arrangements with the race directors Jacques Goddet and Félix Lévitan. Richard Langridge from the British Embassy in Paris was there to smooth the way.

Palmer suggested a stage that would show off Dartmoor but says: 'Goddet and Lévitan took the decision on which course it was to be. Bear in mind this was only one stage and everything had to be moved back to France the moment the stage was completed.'

Among Palmer's collection of memorabilia that he kept as a reminder of the Tour's visit was a letter from the Pedal Club inviting him to give a speech at their luncheon at the Strand Palace Hotel in July 1974, a week after the race had been and gone.

'I was advised that the talk should last twenty minutes,' he says. 'I can't remember much about it but I must have had quite a job to restrict myself to that time.'

One of his most treasured possessions was given to him by JB 'Jock' Wadley, the doyen of cycling writers. 'I had the opportunity to meet with Jock in the build-up to the Tour and he was kind enough to present me with a copy of his book *My Nineteenth Tour de France,* which he signed *To Alf Palmer, who knows more about some aspects of the Tour de France than JBW.*'

Afterwards, Palmer returned to organising his

club's twenty-five-mile time trial and is still a member
of the St Budeaux CC today.

* * *

Posters advertising the Tour's day trip to Plymouth
were distributed to railway and bus stations all over
the country but it could not be said that the race
captured the imagination, except among the hard-
core cycling fans. In mainland Europe, the 1974 race
had been built up as a showdown between the great
Belgian Eddy Merckx, the four-time winner, and the
previous year's champion, Luis Ocaña of Spain.

The fact that Ocaña missed the chance to defend his
crown because of a crash in the Midi-Libre stage race
a few weeks beforehand would not have discouraged
curious British spectators from travelling to Devon.
Very few, if any, cyclists were household names.

The 1974 Tour was to cover 4,107 kilometres, a
good six or seven hundred kilometres longer than the
race is today. Thirteen ten-man teams made up the
130-rider peloton, which is small by today's standards.
And the Tour's route took the riders from Brittany,
via Devon, and then in a clockwise direction around
France, hitting the Alps and then the Pyrenees, culminating on the track at La Cipale in the Parisian suburb
of Vincennes. It was the last year before the Tour's
regular grand finale on the Champs-Élysées.

Merckx won the 7.1-kilometre prologue time trial in Brest on Thursday, 27 June, to take the first yellow jersey of the race.

The following day's opening road stage, from Brest to Saint-Pol-de-Léon, started early, at 8 a.m., and was relatively short, at just 144 kilometres so that the race was finished by around midday.

Italy's Ercole Gualazzini won the stage from Joseph Bruyère of Belgium, and it was Bruyère who took the race lead and would have the honour of becoming the first cyclist to wear the Tour's *maillot jaune* in England.

Three hours after the stage finished, the first of three French air force planes carrying the riders, officials and press landed at Exeter airport. Others working on the race had to cross by ferry and arrived much later in the evening.

Cycling editor Ken Evans was at Exeter airport to see the Tour arrive. Merckx was the first to appear at the aeroplane's door and as he walked down the steps, he allowed his knees to buckle a little, as if to say: 'I'm glad that trip is over.'

Coaches were on hand to take the riders to the Holiday Inn in Plymouth, where a small group of autograph hunters – smaller than we'd expected – were waiting. Soon the hotel lobby was full of stars past and present. There were famous riders who were now managers, including Federico Bahamontes, the 1959 Tour winner nicknamed the Eagle of Toledo, and Briek Schotte, the Bulldog of Flanders. Dutch superstar Fedor den Hertog, a former winner of the Milk Race, asked us where he could buy an umbrella, and others wanted to know where they could change their money from French francs into pounds.

Later, the rest of the Tour entourage arrived, with more journalists, officials, the team cars and their staff and part of the publicity caravan, although most of it remained in France.

The British police were introduced to their French counterparts, including sixteen members of the *garde républicaine,* the president's own escort which always covers Le Tour, and would do so in Plymouth, *sans* their guns, of course.

Pernod, the makers of the aniseed liqueur, hosted a reception for Tour officials at Plymouth town hall. The riders were probably all asleep but not Alf Palmer, who was double-checking the fine detail before the big day.

* * *

The morning dawned dry and bright. Ken Evans and I headed to the circuit, he to the start-finish area where the teams would gather before the race, me to the grandstand that had been constructed near to the finish line. We were both eagerly awaiting the 10 a.m. start of the 163.7-kilometre stage.

Dotted around the course was seating for 5,000 people, with a seat costing £2. There was also standing room for 75,000 but we pretty soon realised that the crowds were not going to be as big as we hoped. The start–finish area at the Deep Lane flyover junction was filling up as buses shuttled spectators from the town, dropping them off around the circuit.

The flyover would be a good vantage point because it would take the riders up and over the dual carriageway on to the other side of the road. The crowds were thin midway down the course at Plympton Hills and Gables Bridge and at the Marsh Mills roundabout, the closest point to Plymouth, where the bunch would reach forty-five miles an hour before they turned at the bottom end of the circuit.

Nevertheless, there was a buzz in the air and the sun was shining on the Tour. You couldn't have wished for better weather.

The finishing-straight banner was in English and French: Start. *Départ*. Finish. *Arrivée*. It also carried the names of sponsoring newspapers from each side of the channel, *Le Parisien* and the *Daily Mirror*. The catering was distinctly British – hamburgers, hot dogs and soft drinks – and there were also tents serving beer.

The atmosphere built, with a military band providing very British pomp and ceremony. The Tour's publicity vehicles passed out cups of tea and Stella

Artois beer, and hats sponsored by the tyre manu-
facturer Michelin. Then came a vintage fire engine
carrying men dressed in the roly-poly Michelin Man
suits, then a truck loaded with artichokes which the
girls threw to a slightly bemused crowd. Finally came
a Parisian bus with a Gallic jazz band on board with
smart young men serving Pernod. The area roped
off for the press and VIPs was full of fans who had
managed to get official accreditation from who knows
where.

And then, at last, came the moment we'd been
waiting for – a riot of colour and sparkling machines,
the sun glinting off the shiny chrome – as 130 of the
world's top riders rolled into view behind the Tour
director's lead car. The crowd broke into spontaneous
applause and, as they drew closer, the applause turned
to cheers. The Tour came alive.

The huge peloton was escorted by the French police
motorcycle outriders and was trailed by a line of team
cars, then press motorbikes and other official vehicles.
For me it was a magnificent sight, for others it was
more bemusing. I heard someone nearby gasp and
then, pointing to the team cars with roof racks decked
out with spare bikes and wheels, compare them to
giant toasters. I guessed he was new to cycling.

Suddenly, we were no longer on a bland dual carriageway in southern England, but in the midst of one
of the world's finest and most spectacular sporting

events. All the fun of the Gallic fair was in the air.

As I watched the bunch assemble ready for the race, I looked through *Cycling* magazine's special Tour issue to familiarise myself with the team jerseys. I could pick out Eddy Merckx, who was not wearing his brown Molteni team jersey but was in the white jersey as leader of the combined competition, which rewarded consistency in the general, points and king of the mountains classifications. Seeing Merckx was a particular thrill, because I knew I was witnessing one of the greats. The Muhammad Ali of cycling. He was favourite to win the Tour and equal Jacques Anquetil's record of five overall victories. He had already won the Giro d'Italia a month earlier after a spring dogged by illness.

Near Merckx was the yellow jersey, the *maillot jaune*, of Jos Bruyère, who led his teammate by sixteen seconds overall. Bernard Thévenet, the best French prospect, was just behind Merckx, wearing the Peugeot team jersey, which was white with a band of black checks around the chest. He had been second overall and won two stages in 1973.

Also in the pack was the most popular rider in France, Raymond Poulidor, nicknamed 'The Eternal Second' after his many close, but unsuccessful, battles with Anquetil. He was the Gan-Mercier team's best hope of victory.

Right alongside Poulidor was his Gan teammate,

then Britain's most prolific Tour stage winner Barry Hoban. As soon as we saw Hoban we clapped, cheered and called his name.

Hoban's sunburnt face broadened into a big smile and he waved back. For him this must have been an extra special moment, to be riding a Tour stage on home ground. Earlier in the season, he'd won the Ghent–Wevelgem Classic in Belgium, followed by a smaller one-day race, Paris–Bourges. He had won his first Tour stage in 1967, when he was allowed to go clear of the bunch the day after Tom Simpson had died to pay tribute to his teammate. Hoban won another stage in 1968, two in 1969 and two in 1973. We hoped Hoban could win in Plymouth, and why not? He was one of the fastest sprinters in the bunch but he perhaps preferred tougher terrain to this.

There were other fast men, including the only other British rider in the field, Essex-born Michael Wright, who had lived in Belgium from an early age and had trouble speaking English but was nevertheless one of our own. Wright was riding for the Sonolor-Gitane team and had won three stages, in 1965, 1967 and 1973. Then there was the Flemish Arrow, the Belgian Patrick Sercu, wearing the distinctive American-themed red, white and blue colours of the team sponsored by Brooklyn chewing gum.

Sercu was well known to British cycling fans as three-time winner of the Skol Six-Day at Wembley.

He was also handy on the road, as three stage wins at the Giro proved.

The officials were celebrities in our eyes too – especially the two men who ran the Tour, Jacques Goddet and Félix Lévitan. We saw Goddet emerge from a bright red Peugeot lead car, bristling with radio aerials, just near the start line. The headboard on the car bore the *Daily Mirror*'s red title piece, as they were sponsors of the stage.

The excitement continued to build and the sight of the British bobbies alongside the French *gendarmes* signified this *entente cordiale*.

At last, with a roar from the motorcycle engines, and shouts of encouragement from the crowd, the stage got underway. The lead cars accelerated clear to give the big field space, a helicopter's blades clattered overhead and the team cars that followed the riders tootled their sing-song horns.

Then all that could be heard was the murmur of the crowd as the Tour disappeared over the brow of the hill. It would be around fifteen to seventeen minutes before they returned.

For those of us who understood the nuances of bike racing, we knew that a dual carriageway was not the place for a rider to beat their brains out trying to escape from the pack. Firstly, they would never be able to escape the view of their chasers, making it almost impossible to tease out a winning advantage.

As expected, the course was not tough enough to split the field, especially not this early in the Tour, with three weeks still to go.

So the organisers had livened things up by dangling a few juicy carrots in front of the riders. There were eight £100 *prime* sprints and at the end of laps six and ten there were hot-spot sprints that carried a time bonus that would be deducted from the rider's overall time. Merckx led the hot-spots competition overall, with Hoban equal second with Gerben Karstens, a Dutch rider. With the field knowing there was cash to be won, they had to be vigilant when the attacks came.

All this was lost on the newcomers who, perhaps like a Frenchman at a test match, couldn't understand the finer points.

On one of the closing laps, when the whole Bic team screamed past us at full pelt a few hundred yards off the back of the bunch, my neighbours in the grandstand could not understand why. I explained to them that their top sprinter, Karstens, had probably punctured, so his teammates had dropped back to pace him up to the field. What we saw was the Bic team lined out, with the front man riding as hard as possible before peeling off and letting the next man set the pace. The idea, I said, was to get Karstens back to the bunch within five kilometres so he'd have time to recover from the effort before the sprint finish. It meant his teammates riding with their eyes on stalks at more than forty miles an hour. My neighbours were impressed with my knowledge.

Disappointingly, only one of the commentators describing the race over the public address system did a decent job of relaying the action to the crowd. Perhaps they weren't getting enough information about what was going on in the race. The guys on the microphones were all linked up along the course and, as the on-course commentators do at the Grand National, they would commentate as the race was in their section before handing on to the next guy as the race left their field of view. Only one commentator, Phil Liggett, was on the ball, telling of the attacks as they played out.

So, how did it all play out?

Well, it was fast. And Hoban, perhaps sensing that his best chance of victory would come from a smaller group, quickly went on the attack but he was a marked man on home ground and was not allowed to get away.

The field remained intact for the first lap and returned into sight, rolling slickly by on the opposite carriageway, up the slip road to encircle the roundabout before belting down the other slip road to pass me in the stands, fanning out into *echelon* formation as the stiff breeze blew across the road.

Every few laps the pace would shoot up as each

£100 *prime* beckoned. To our delight, the two Brits got stuck in. Hoban took one £100 *prime*, was third in the first hot-spot sprint and won the second. Wright also won two *primes*.

The Michelin *prime* on the second lap was taken by Spain's José Pesarrodona of the Kas team. Aussie Don Allan of Frisol took the Raleigh *prime* on lap three and attempted to stay clear, in vain.

Then Hoban chanced his arm again, taking the Debenhams *prime* on the fifth lap. There was alarm in the Lejeune team when Daniel Ducreux fell, but he soon rejoined the bunch, helped by teammates.

There was excitement as Sercu hit the front as they passed the grandstands, the Brooklyn star leading the long string across the line.

Eagerly we scanned the pack, spotting white-clad Merckx surrounded by his Molteni team, keen to keep everything running smoothly, steadily, all under control.

It all speeded up on the sixth lap as a Dutchman pressed harder on the pedals at the approach of the hot-spot sprint. The field, knowing vital seconds were at stake, snaked after him in one long line. Now they really got moving, as Cees Bal of Gan-Mercier managed to get a hundred-metre lead as they sped out of our sight. His teammates tried – fruitlessly – to hold back the chase and Bal was brought to heel two kilometres later.

Not to be put off, Gan attacked again when their

man Gerard Vianen took off, with Jean-Claude Blocher (Jobo-Lejeune) for company. The field was having none of it and quickly pulled them back. Well, it took back Blocher, but Vianen had the nerve to keep going – for a little longer. He nearly made it to the line, but was swamped in the gallop and it was Bic's Karstens who snatched this first hot-spot sprint, just in front of Merckx and Hoban.

All these Gan attacks had speeded up the race, which clocked fifteen minutes for the lap, at an average of nearly fifty kilometres per hour. Hoban and Herman Van Springel (MIC-De Gribaldy) kept it going, getting clear for a couple of kilometres. Things were hotting up, as Wright put his nose out in front for the Aspro-Nicholas *prime*. He took it with a twelve-second lead and kept going.

Now the Molteni team took over, a sea of brown jerseys flooding the front of the pack to give chase, bringing Wright back by the end of the lap.

Sercu had a rapid bike change and Wright attacked again at the end of the eighth lap, taking the Accolade *prime* with a ten-second advantage over two chasers, Michel Coroller (Merlin Plage-Shimano) and Wilfried David (Flandria-Carpenter), with the main field at eighteen seconds.

It was all too close to call. The field – and especially Merckx's Molteni team – was having none of it.

Back they all came, as the 'King' himself took the

race by the scruff of the neck and led the field over the line on both laps eight and nine, with one to go for the second hot-spot sprint.

Up went the pace again, which was bad news for Portugal's Oliveira who crashed and would never regain the field. Merckx went for the bonus, but it was not to be as first Karstens went past him, and then so did Hoban who took the sprint in a photo finish.

Then Bal again got stuck in, to the annoyance of the Molteni riders who had just seen their master beaten by Bal's teammate Hoban!

Meanwhile, Karstens suddenly stopped at the road-side with a flat tyre, meaning that his Bic team faced the double whammy of pacing him back while the field ahead had split and was in full flight chasing Bal.

And while all this was going on, Hoban found himself in the second group. He was forced to put in a backbreaking effort to get back to the front group, which was being led by Merckx and his men. No one wanted to help Hoban out, so he had to do the bulk of the work himself. There were now twelve laps done, two to go.

The pace was red hot as attack followed attack, with all of them snuffed out under the orders of the yellow jersey himself, Bruyère, and Merckx.

Into the final lap and Mariano Martínez (Sonolor), Gerrie Knetemann (Gan-Mercier) and Marc Demeyer (Flandria-Carpenter) were among the big names to attack, all to no avail.

Cyrille Guimard (Merlin-Plage) crashed – landing heavily on his hip. His teammate Van Landeghem waited for him, and the pair would finish six minutes down.

Ahead of them, the whole field regrouped, and it was again in one long line as they tore up and over the roundabout for the last time, heading for the finish.

And out of the heaving mass of the 124-man bunch sprint, came the blond mop of Dutchman Henk Poppe, still only twenty-one until his birthday the following week. So it was that Poppe snatched a brilliant victory in his first year as a pro. He'd spotted Merckx, who appeared to be leading out Sercu, despite him being on a rival team!

'I heard Merckx shout to Sercu, so I stuck to them and when a gap opened, I went through,' said an ecstatic Poppe who took some famous scalps in his career. Jacques Esclassan (Peugeot) was second, Sercu third, Hoban ninth. Poppe was no stranger to our shores, having ridden the Milk Race.

'I was boxed in,' said Hoban. 'I was a bit of an idiot, I suppose. I tried too hard early on and in the finish didn't quite have it. Naturally everyone knew I would be out to win in my own country and I was watched all the time.'

He added that normally he wouldn't make such a big effort this early in the Tour. 'But the crowd was so marvellous. I really do appreciate their support.'

And so that was that. The greatest day in the history of road cycling in the UK was over and the Tour made ready to return to France. Fans lingered on as the Tour bikes were placed in special protective carriers before being loaded on to lorries. The riders piled into coaches for a trip to the showers, and then Exeter airport.

Merckx was the last to board his coach, delayed by autograph hunters and others wanting to talk, or just to stare.

And three hours later, the A38 was getting back to normal.

Meanwhile, the customs officers at Exeter had the last word, insisting on going through every rider's bag individually, laboriously, delaying them two hours longer than was really necessary.

As a result, the riders didn't get to their hotels in France until 10 p.m.

As Ken Evans wrote: 'Plymouth's great and largely successful efforts may well have been ruined by that officiousness. It will probably be a long time before we see the Tour again.'

Twenty years, to be precise.

Keith Bingham is the former Chief Reporter at *Cycling Weekly*, and retired recently after a record 40 years' service. A pioneer of cycling comment, he has covered the Tour de France, the Continental Classics, World Championships, the Tours of Britain and a multitude of home events.

8

Just what did happen to Basque pro
rider Iban Mayo after he retired?
Didn't he become a long-distance
lorry driver?

Richard Moore sits down for lunch
– a very long, well-lubricated lunch –
with a rider who was once capable of
pushing Lance Armstrong to his limits,
and discovers a sensitive soul who
enjoyed a racing career of ups
and downs, but who now enjoys
life off the bike even more.

THE LONG-DISTANCE
LORRY DRIVER*

BY RICHARD MOORE

These days, Iban Mayo is a long-distance lorry driver.

It was one of the lines that jumped out of Tyler Hamilton's book, *The Secret Race*. Which is saying something, because attention-grabbing revelations were hardly in short supply, from motorcycle EPO couriers to blood bags fixed to coat hangers to botched transfusions . . . despite all that, a revelation about a relatively obscure and six-years-retired Basque climber managed to pique people's curiosity. It certainly piqued mine.

There was something poignant about it, too. Iban Mayo, who blazed as brightly as his orange Euskaltel jersey for two seasons, in 2003 and 2004, might have been the heir to Marco Pantani, with all that implies. He had the same build, the same electrifying ability to go uphill fast, perhaps the same demons and mental fragility, too. As much as we remember Mayo's win at Alpe d'Huez in the 2003 Tour de France, or his record ascent of Mont Ventoux during the 2004

Dauphiné, and his demolition, on both occasions, of Lance Armstrong, we recall his collapse at the 2004 Tour, on the road to Plateau de Beille.

It should have been a triumph: hundreds of thousands of his people – orange-clad Basques – awaited Mayo on the mountain, fully expecting him to put Armstrong to the sword. But he cracked. He was dropped even before they reached the big climbs. He tried to climb off his bike, only to be forced back on by teammates. This was a collapse that seemed, to the lay observer, psychological as much as physical: a mid-race meltdown. It was painful to watch, and must have been humiliating for Mayo.

And it seemed that he never fully recovered from that. Shades of Pantani again. Struggling to cope with the attention and pressure that came with leading Euskaltel-Euskadi – at the height of his fame Mayo was reportedly offered a 'five-figure sum' to pose nude for *Interviú* magazine – he did the unthinkable and moved away from the Basque Country and its obsession with cycling, and with him. He turned up next in the bright yellow of Saunier Duval, the Spanish team that for its brief life seemed like a refuge for outcasts and misfits, renegades and redemption-seekers, from Mayo to Riccardo Riccò, Leonardo Piepoli to David Millar, who was returning from his two-year doping ban. (To illustrate what a broad and inclusive church it was, the Italian Marco Pinotti, later a vocal proponent of clean cycling, also spent two years at Saunier Duval.)

For Mayo, there was a stage win at the Giro d'Italia in Saunier Duval colours in 2007, but he tested positive for EPO at the Tour de France a couple of months later. Unusually, the B-sample was declared inconclusive, only for Pat McQuaid, then the UCI president, to demand a re-test. This confirmed the original analysis. Mayo complained of a witch hunt, appealed, lost, then disappeared. And that was him finished with cycling. Still only thirty, he dropped out of the picture. His subsequent silence was difficult to interpret. But it seemed, once again adopting Pantani as the blueprint, ominous.

Iban Mayo, the swashbuckling Basque climber, who with his straggly shoulder-length hair and hooped earrings had something of the indie rock star about him, lurked in many cycling fans' subconscious. There had always been something appealing about him; he was, as Dan Coyle wrote in *Tour de Force*, 'a sharp-edged mix of beauty and arrogance' who 'seemed to inhabit a waking dream, floating slightly above the world'. There was a mystique about him, an other-worldly quality, that might have owed rather a lot to the proud, insular, impenetrable region he was from. As Coyle pithily claimed: '"Because he is Basque" was the answer to most questions about Iban Mayo.'

Faint memories of Mayo were triggered by his

mention in Hamilton's book (ghost-written by Coyle). A long-distance lorry driver, eh? It made sense. The long hours, the loneliness of the road, eating alone in motorway service stations, sleeping in his cabin in deserted laybys, maybe picking up hitchhikers and telling them about his previous life as a professional cyclist. Or maybe not.

If you thought about it, the life of the long-distance lorry driver would have many parallels with that of a professional cyclist. Especially climbers, those loners in search of escape and solitude: 'Individualists, brave, stubborn, cerebral, hypochondriacal and lonely,' as Roger Kahn describes baseball pitchers in *The Boys of Summer*.

Clearly I wasn't the only one fascinated by Mayo, and in particular by the idea of him criss-crossing Europe alone in his lorry, his glory days receding in the rear-view mirror until they were a tiny speck, hardly visible. Do a Google search for 'Iban Mayo' and Autofill offers three options: 'doping', 'Ventoux' and 'truck driver'.

There is only one problem: Iban Mayo was not, and indeed never has been, a long-distance lorry driver.

* * *

Remarkably, nobody seemed to know what he was doing. I asked some Spanish contacts, but nothing. Then again, the fact he was an enigma when he was

racing perhaps meant that it was logical that he would
be elusive in retirement. But some weeks after my initial inquiries there was an email from Eneko Garate,
who managed another Basque team, Kaiku, and now
runs Libros de Ruta, a Bilbao-based publisher of
cycling books.

Eneko said that a local journalist, Alain Laiseka,
knew Mayo, and was still in touch with him. I made
contact with Alain and he said he'd speak to Mayo.
It was a few months before I heard from him again,
when he emailed to say he had spoken to Mayo, who
had – to my surprise, and possibly Alain's, too – agreed
to an interview. But on one condition: 'He doesn't
want to speak about today's polemics in cycling.'

So here I am, on a freezing cold December day
in Bilbao, about to meet Iban Mayo. But first I meet
Alain in a bar in the old town. Dark-haired and
dishevelled, with a scruffy beard, Alain is a thirty-
six-year-old with good English and an equally good
sense of cynical humour, and over coffee he tells me
the plan. We are meeting Mayo a few hours later in
another bar. He has booked lunch in a restaurant
down by the Nervión river. Then Alain tells me a bit
about Mayo – emphasis on 'bit', because he doesn't
seem to know too much. They are the same age and
raced together as juniors. 'Well, not together,' Alain
clarifies. Once the races got underway, Mayo was
gone: he was a phenomenal junior.

So what about this story of Mayo as a lorry driver. Was it ever true? Alain laughs and shakes his head. Then he turns more serious. 'Iban is very shy. Or . . . not shy. That is not the right word.'

'Cagey? Guarded?'

'Yes,' Alain nods vigorously. 'He does not trust people he does not know.'

Alain heads off to his work on the sports desk at *Deia*, his newspaper, leaving me to think about Mayo, how he might have aged and how difficult it might be to win his trust over lunch. My uncertainty is heightened by the fact that the previous week I had interviewed his old adversary, Armstrong, for a book. Talking to Armstrong, there were two names that provoked an impassioned, not to mention angry, response. One was Travis Tygart, the head of the US Anti-Doping Agency. The other was Mayo.

Armstrong recalled the 2003 Dauphiné Libéré, in which he crashed and was in a bad way. His team wanted him to pull out. 'But Iban Mayo was in second,' Armstrong told me. 'And, let me tell you, I was not a fan. I was not a fan of Mayo. I thought he was a little punk. We were all sort of . . . dirty, but I viewed him as being a lot dirtier than us.' When Michele Ferrari advised Armstrong to withdraw, he said: 'No way, because if I go home this punk wins.

'So I stayed in, and he kept attacking me, attacking me hard over the Galibier. And it just fucking killed me to stay with him . . . but I wasn't going to let this little punk win.'

To this day, Armstrong believes that Mayo – or more accurately, his battle with him at the Dauphiné – is the reason he began the 2003 Tour below par.

At 2 p.m. I meet Alain again. We stand by the bar, each nursing a beer, keeping an eye on the door. Two o'clock comes and goes. But a few minutes later there's a burst of orange and a figure enters. He wears a shiny (Euskaltel-orange) puffa jacket with fur-lined hood, smart dark slim-fit jeans, new black trainers. His hair is thinning on top, longish and straggly at the back; he has a long, sharp nose and immaculately styled stubble that is almost a beard: unmistakably Iban Mayo.

He smiles shyly and makes fleeting eye contact as he shakes my hand, then turns to the bar and orders a glass of red wine, swilling it carefully in the glass before sipping, equally carefully. He begins talking to Alain, a torrent of words. Mayo appears edgy and fidgety, yet at the same time relaxed and confident. We finish our drinks, and move on. But not to lunch – not yet. To another bar first. 'This is lunch in the Basque Country,' Alain explains.

In the second bar a stranger approaches. Has he recognised the former cyclist? No, he knows Alain, and while they talk I try to communicate with Mayo. Is he recognised often? He shakes his head. 'In 2003, 2004, yes. Now, no.'

At the mention of his cycling career, and his fame at its peak, he laughs in a detached way, as though it was something that happened to someone else. 'Crazy,' he says, pointing at his head. 'But cyclists are a little bit crazy.'

'Do you drive a lorry?' I ask Mayo. He looks confused. 'A truck?' I try to mimic holding a large steering wheel. Alain rejoins us and translates. 'No,' says Mayo, 'I have an electrical installation company.' (This makes sense. Before he turned professional, he trained as an electrician.)

He adds, 'Do you need electrical installation in Scotland?'

Finally we arrive at Miren Itziar, our restaurant, close to the old market of La Ribera: a dark, underground, cavernous space. There's a bar on the way in, and we pause here for a third aperitif. The barman thinks he recognises the athletic-looking figure in the orange jacket, so Alain invites him to guess who it is. 'A footballer?' he asks. Mayo seems to enjoy the fact that the barman knows his face, but can't remember his name.

At 3.30 we sit down for lunch. As we're handed menus, Mayo orders two bottles of red wine. Then he hands the waiter his phone and asks him to take a picture of the three of us. I am sitting beside Mayo with Alain opposite, and throughout lunch – which will stretch to three-and-a-half hours – Mayo keeps

picking up his phone and checking it. I keep trying to
see what he is doing – checking on his business perhaps? – but eventually realise that he's on Facebook.
He's uploaded the picture of our lunch party and is
checking the comments underneath.

'Having lunch with Alain Laiseka and a Scottish
journalist,' Mayo had written.

'Behave, the Scott [*sic*] looks pissed [off],' someone
has commented underneath.

'Don't worry bro, he'll have a whisky afterwards
and he'll calm down.'

* * *

The two bottles of wine arrive, and the first plate of
food: 'Fritos variados de la casa'. A large plate over-
flowing with fried food. That'll cheer the Scotsman
up.

I tell Mayo that I want to start at the beginning:
that I understand he was a welder's son who grew up
in the small village of Igorre; and that when he was
very young he was good at football and basketball.
'The thing is,' he says, 'that when I was a kid I was
a bad student, and I was always getting into scrapes,
falling down and injuring myself. And my parents
said, "Well, if you like being out and about so much,
at the very least, do a sport that involves you being
outdoors." So I started playing [the Basque game]

pelota aged ten or so, but when I was eleven or twelve for some reason there weren't any games in my category round where I lived, so I got bored being stuck indoors again and switched to football.

'That was okay, but I was really bad at football. So I went through a spell of athletics and karate, and finally I got into cycling by chance because some friends I'd hang out with a lot used to ride bikes. And I wasn't very good at it at first. I would get dropped after a few laps, but I liked the atmosphere at races; they'd give you a sandwich, you'd get to ride on buses to races. But I was bad at everything. Most of the races were twelve laps and in my first I was dropped after six, and it was curious, I was completely alone and people watching didn't realise that I was actually out the back, they thought I was leading . . .' Mayo laughs, then continues, barely pausing for breath. 'But that was just the first race, and after that things improved pretty fast. By the fourth or fifth I was getting second or third, then I started winning once or twice, and that was even though we didn't use racing bikes much. As a young teenager I didn't have one at home so they'd be loaned to us by the club twice a week and we'd be allowed to train on them for two days . . .'

Mayo joined a local club, Sociedad Ciclista Arrate. Then he caught the eye of the national selectors, and in 1995 he was selected for the junior World Championships in San Moritz. The road race was dominated by the Italians, who swept the first three places: Valentino China taking gold, Ivan Basso silver and Rinaldo Nocentini bronze. Mayo was fourth. (China was the only one who didn't go on to greater things: he rode for three seasons with Mario Cipollini at Saeco, but was no longer a professional by twenty-five. He was last heard of working for a shipping company near Bergamo.)

The junior Worlds in San Moritz were an eye-opener for Mayo. 'I was impressed by the way the other riders trained. In my local squad, we'd do a couple of hours and then go to the beach. These foreigners, the Italians and Russians, were training so hard for hours, riding high tempo behind cars – that surprised me. They were more professional than me.'

As for turning professional himself, 'I didn't know,' Mayo says. 'You dream of it. I thought I was forging a good path for myself, with fourth in the Worlds and so on . . . Well, you think about it as possible, that if you go on like that then something could come of it. There was a long way to go, but that was my dream. I'd won a lot of races, more than twenty.' Alain, sitting opposite, nods in confirmation.

By nineteen he was riding for the amateur Banesto team and there was only one hurdle for Mayo to negotiate before turning pro: national service. As a conscientious objector, Mayo became an ambulance driver with the Red Cross. 'That way,' he says, 'I could stay at home and go on training.' But one afternoon, 'I was on duty from three until ten, I'd finished training and I was driving my own car, taking it to the Red Cross for a car wash, and I lost concentration when I was looking for something in the car.

'I was looking on the back seat for a set of keys and when I turned back round I was driving into a wall. I smashed open my elbow, I hurt my head and my legs were trapped and hurting like hell. I didn't lose consciousness but I had terrible pain everywhere. So a woman who was nearby called up the firemen and an ambulance, which included people I worked with. And one of my workmates managed to disentangle my legs by unblocking my shoes from where they were trapped in the chassis. I'll never forget the pain.'

Both his legs were broken. 'I was in hospital for all of August and halfway through September. My legs were in plaster, my face was all beaten up, I didn't have a broken collarbone but my shoulder was swollen up and my arm was in plaster, too. I was in a wheelchair until December.'

Mayo pulls up his sleeve to reveal the pale white scar on his right arm, almost glowing in the dim restaurant. At no point, he says, did he consider that his accident meant the end of his cycling ambitions. 'No. In fact, the minute I was out of plaster and out of the wheelchair, I couldn't walk, but the first thing I did, without telling anybody, was try to ride my bike. It

was incredible, because my leg muscles were all sof-
tened up after all those months; they felt like they
were as bendy as hosepipes. My cycling clothes were
baggy because my legs had lost muscle mass and were
a lot thinner.'

Banesto didn't want to know, though. 'The minute
I had the accident they told me not only that I wasn't
going to be turning pro, but I was out of the team.'
Mayo was contacted by Sabino Angoitia, a former
Basque professional, who was *directeur sportif* at another
team, Cafés Baqué. 'So I went there for a year, and it
was very hard building up the muscle again so it wasn't a
great year, but bearing in mind what had happened, not
so bad. And then the next year things got a lot better.'

* * *

The fritos have been polished off and the plate is
whisked away just in time for the next one to arrive:
sea clams in a rich, creamy sauce. Mayo opens the
second bottle of wine.

He joined Euskaltel in 2000, when he was twenty-two. The following year he won Midi Libre and
the Classique des Alpes. Here, clearly, was the latest
graduate of the Basque school of climbing, whose
alumni included Marino Lejarreta, Federico Echave,
Iñaki Gastón, Julián Gorospe, Abraham Olano, Pello
Ruiz Cabestany, the list goes on.

But Mayo didn't think he was a natural climber. 'It was more that I liked the climbing when I was watching the mountain stages of races on the TV, and what you see is what you'd like to be. I could pretty much do anything as a junior – time trialling, climbing, sprinting, but the mountains were what everybody liked the best, and so did I, and as I liked it, so I wanted to do well in those stages.' He liked Indurain, of course, 'but I was more a fan of Chiappucci, Marino [Lejaretta], or Delgado, who would attack and then almost immediately crack. I loved the way he would try so hard, dig really deep, get dropped, then get back on.

'I was more a fan of spectacular racing than results. It was all very emotional. I was a fan of Pantani but the problem is once you turn pro and race alongside them, they're no longer as special to you. They lose their shine.'

It was 2003, and his Dauphiné duel with Armstrong, that brought Mayo wider attention. I wonder, was he aware that he got under Armstrong's skin? 'I remember the look he gave me. But not only that, the last day we were chasing down Mancebo and Millar on the climbs coming into Grenoble, and I was really giving it everything. I'd attacked every day that week; I swear to you, those attacks, not even Froome could have followed them. And on the last day Armstrong came up to me, drew level with my

handlebars and said to me, "Iban, can't you go a bit
harder than that?" So that day I went so hard we went
past Millar and Mancebo and Armstrong came up to
me again and said, "Is that all you've got? Can't you
go any harder?" And so we'd do it all over again and
again, each time Armstrong asking me, "Can't you go
any harder?" and me attacking again.'

Did he think he could beat him at the Tour? 'No,'
Mayo replies. 'I had the form of my life, but no, he
was on another level. I'd had a very good year, starting
in the Vuelta País Vasco and then in Liège–Bastogne–
Liège, but I knew he would be better than me in the
Tour. He had the level, he had the team, he had the
time trials: it was nice to be up there fighting with him
in the Dauphiné, but the Tour is different . . . okay, I
got second overall at the Dauphiné, and the guy who
was third was a long way behind me and Armstrong,
but the difference between Armstrong and the rest of
us was enormous. He was way superior to the rest.'

Yet Armstrong was worried about Mayo. 'People
told me afterwards,' Mayo shrugs. 'Maybe I was more
unpredictable than Ullrich. I could attack on other
climbs, because I could go all out in one place or
another whereas Ullrich would not surprise him, he'd
be a guy who would go for him in the time trials. But
really you're not thinking about that, you're thinking
about your own objectives. Maybe with a big attack
I could get rid of his team, cut things down to three

or four riders in the mountains – me, Ullrich, him, Basso and who knows who else. I could surprise him, but not to win the Tour.'

But he had his moments, the biggest being on Alpe d'Huez in that 2003 Tour. In a classic Armstrong bluff, he sought to camouflage his weakness by instructing his team, US Postal Service, to set a brutal pace at the base of the mountain. 'It was a long flat approach, then over the Galibier,' Mayo remembers, 'then at the foot of the Alpe d'Huez, US Postal went really hard. We were all thinking this was the year that maybe Armstrong wasn't as good as in other Tours. I was actually in trouble on the lower part; I didn't think continuing at that speed was possible. But then I got back up to the group after about six hundred metres, where they were going flat out with Triki [Manuel] Beltrán. But then it slowed a bit after it had come down to Heras, Armstrong, Beloki, Hamilton and me.' Beloki attacked. He was a danger – second the previous year – and Armstrong rode hard to bring him back. Then there was a lull. 'And I thought, "Now's your chance",' says Mayo. 'I attacked, I went for it, nobody followed. It was a long way out, maybe seven kilometres from the summit, and I just went for it steadily.'

It wasn't a plan? 'Yes, but it's always the same: everybody talks about plans but only you know when you're feeling good enough to follow it. I knew that it was the right moment to attack. I thought that the

only person strong enough to follow me would be
Armstrong and why would he want to do that when
his main interest was in controlling Beloki and the
rest? I attacked because it was the moment. If I hadn't
gone then, I would have done later, but at the same
time attacking is often a question of having this' –
Mayo gestures at his crotch: his balls – 'and knowing
it's the right moment rather than feeling strong.'

Behind, Armstrong was heavy-legged, hesitant,
and didn't commit to the chase: not the Armstrong
of the previous four Tours. He could afford to give
Mayo a bit of rope – the Basque was almost four minutes down, having, predictably, lost three in the team
time trial. But high on the Alpe, with three kilometres
to go, Mayo, his orange Euskaltel jersey wide open
and flapping like a superhero's cape, knew he was
going to win. He was 1min45secs ahead of Alexandr
Vinokourov at the summit, with Armstrong third,
another thirty seconds back. It was a convincing victory, one that Mayo celebrated in exuberant fashion,
zipping up his jersey, waving at the packed crowds,
smiling, biting his bottom lip as though to stop himself laughing. He seemed to enjoy it.

Does he ever watch it on YouTube? 'Yes.'

His 2003 Tour wasn't finished. Mayo was involved
in one of the most infamous incidents of Armstrong's
Tour career, when Armstrong was pulled from his bike
on Luz Ardiden, after catching a child's *musette* with

his handlebars. Mayo was following and went down too, landing on top of the American. He was up first, but was almost brought down again when Armstrong's chain jumped. As Armstrong lurched forward, Mayo almost went into the back of him. (Later, Armstrong discovered that his frame had been bent in the crash, most likely because Mayo landed on it.)

Mayo sprinted up the road and rejoined the group before Armstrong regained contact, just as Tyler Hamilton was making a great show of urging Jan Ullrich to slow down and wait. Mayo smirks as he recalls this then waves his hand dismissively. 'Hamilton was saying we should wait for Armstrong. Hamilton wasn't on a good day, that is my impression.'

* * *

Next, *merluza con pimientos rojos*: hake with red peppers. Can't be any better than the clams. Mayo tops up our glasses.

The stage to Plateau de Beille in 2004. The day of his meltdown. That is what I most want to hear about. I was on the mountain with some friends: the last Tour I attended as a fan rather than a journalist. I remember the giddy sense of excitement among the thousands of Basques who, in their orange T-shirts and brandishing their Ikurriñas, choked the approach roads, clogged up the village of Verdun and streamed up the mountain, high on a heady mix of anticipation and alcohol. It was all about Mayo.

Armstrong's popularity was at an all-time low; Mayo's at an all-time high, the 'little punk' having recently kicked the Texan's butt in the time trial up Mont Ventoux at the Dauphiné, setting a new record for the climb (which still stands). As Dan Coyle wrote in *Tour de Force*, Mayo's 'gazelle legs moved faster, the chain hummed, the tiny bike rocked back and forth' as he beat Armstrong by a minute. 'How the fuck was Mayo so fast?' asked Armstrong when he reached his team car. 'Mayo is not superman,' said Johan Bruyneel, Armstrong's director. 'He cannot stay at this level for five more weeks. It is not possible.'

Bruyneel was right. And yet it was impossible – is impossible – to know whether Mayo's 2004 Tour might have panned out differently had it not included cobbles. Stage three to Wasquehal saw him come a cropper on the *pavé*. He finished with a gaping hole in his shorts, and a bloody hole in his hip, over four minutes down. Naturally, when he went down, Armstrong and US Postal took full advantage. 'Almost four minutes for Mayo is a very, very important gap,' said Bruyneel at the finish, stopping just short of rubbing his hands in glee.

After that disaster Mayo fell ill. 'I was fucked,' he says between mouthfuls of hake and red peppers. 'I had glandular fever. I should have got off that day [to Plateau de Beille]. I had been in great form before the

Tour but after falling on the *pavé* early on, and then feeling bad, maybe it had nothing to do with it, but every day I got worse and worse.'

The nadir came on that fateful stage 13 when, on a road that was barely a slope, he dropped back through the convoy, all the way to his team car. Surrounded by teammates, who were trying to coax and cajole him, he looked imploringly at his team car. He slowed, almost stopped, then carried on. It was desperate; almost comical, but also shocking – this was the rider Armstrong feared?

'It wasn't because of my head that I wanted to stop, it was illness,' Mayo says. 'I wanted to abandon, but [teammates] David Etxebarria and Unai Etxebarria convinced me to continue the stage and that we talk afterwards. But I was really bad; I had no energy. It wasn't mental; I had pus building up in my throat, I was suffering badly. And after a flat stage and a rest day I went out to train and I could barely turn the pedals. I said to Miguel [Madariaga, founder and manager of the Euskaltel team] that evening, "I'm fucked, I can't swallow, and I can't eat." And then later Miguel said some stupid things about how I hadn't said goodbye, but that's not true. I did. I went to Galdakao hospital and they diagnosed me with glandular fever and I was at home suffering really badly.'

On Plateau de Beille, the Basque fans parted as the day's winner, Armstrong, motored towards the summit with Ivan Basso in his jetstream. Then they waited for Mayo. And waited. And waited. It was thirty-eight minutes before the sickly Mayo finally appeared.

Now, he says, 'I had created a degree of anticipation and expectation that something could happen. I think a lot of Basque people went to the Tour that year simply because of what they thought I could do. Maybe not win, but at least be a protagonist, though I was trying to play things down.'

The build-up to the Tour had seen the peak of Mayo-mania — and you can't help but wonder at the effect it had on him. 'Unai [Larrea, the Basque journalist who was Alain's predecessor at *Deia*] was on the phone all the time. There were people calling me, magazines, newspapers, it was crazy. At home the doorbell just wouldn't stop ringing. I'd go out training and immediately a motorbike and a photographer would be on my trail. I had no idea how they knew I was out training. I remember it really got to me. I was under a lot of pressure. I had to change my phone number just to stop people calling me all the time. I asked another journalist if Contador had ever been under the same pressure and media interest and they said he wasn't. This was something special.'

At the summit of Plateau de Beille, Mayo told reporters: 'I'm mad because I'm not going good and I don't know why. But it's not the worst day of my life today. I'm only twenty-six and I know there will be more Tours for me in the future.'

There were, and there weren't. In 2005 he did little other than finish a lowly 60th in the Tour. In 2006 he didn't finish at all. And in 2007, now racing for Saunier Duval, and with a Giro stage win after a lone attack on an undulating stage, he was 16th overall before the announcement of his positive test.

***

Dessert has arrived: a gooey, sweet concoction, with the texture of rice pudding.

Mayo wasn't the only Saunier Duval rider to taste success at the 2007 Giro: Riccardo Riccò and Leonardo Piepoli were also stage winners in a race won by Danilo Di Luca. But on the results sheet there are almost as many scored-out names as there are names, yet Mayo's (as well as Riccò's and Piepoli's, who both tested positive the following year) and Di Luca's are still there.

A footnote to Saunier Duval's successes in 2007 was written by David Millar in his book, *Racing Through the Dark*. In his second and final year with the Spanish team, and still to fully reinvent himself as a credible anti-doping campaigner, Millar wrote to the UCI president, Pat McQuaid, highlighting his concerns and suspicions about his own team. He did not receive a reply.

At the time, Millar did not go public with his concerns. On the eve of the 2007 Tour I asked him about Mayo, who intrigued me, and Millar, despite whatever misgivings he might have, couldn't help but smile. 'Who knows what he's capable of? If he's been at home not eating pie, then he could be amazing. He's an incredible bike rider; to do what he did at the Giro was awe-inspiring. I think he's the only bike rider in the world who could win a mountain stage in a Grand Tour three kilos overweight.

'He's a proper little fruit loop but ridiculously gifted,' Millar continued. 'He is very shy, not a very good people person. He's not a people person at all – a loner, really. When he's bad he's really bad. But when he's on fire . . .'

Mayo did not set the 2007 Tour on fire. He did place second, to Michael Rasmussen, at Tignes in the Alps, but he was missing his old spark. Then, after stage 16, he tested positive for EPO. But his case was curious. Initially he seemed to be exonerated. A second test of his sample, at a lab in Ghent, was inconclusive, which was enough for him to be cleared by the Spanish federation. But a reanalysis of his B-sample was ordered by McQuaid (perhaps he had paid some attention to Millar's letter, after all) and in December a French laboratory determined that it did contain EPO: Mayo was guilty after all. He appealed to the Court of Arbitration for Sport but in mid-2008 they confirmed the ruling: he was banned for two years, backdated to July 2009.

But he showed no desire to return when his ban concluded. He was only thirty-two. Did he consider coming back? 'Yes, but I was burned out, disappointed with it all. Why? You know how it was, a series of [doping] controls which went from positive to negative and then they did a final analysis. It was a whole year of fighting and trials and stories and you know what they did . . . a lot of stress. And now I've seen what's happened with Armstrong, and all those stories. People can believe what they like, that I was ashamed, but I was just really burned out and didn't believe in the system any more, and then I've been proved right, because I've seen what happened to Armstrong.'

What does he mean – that Armstrong has been treated unfairly? 'It's very complicated. After what we've seen with Armstrong and now with other riders, like Rasmussen, I think cycling's credibility is below zero right now. I said this before, I simply don't believe in anything. I don't believe in the system, because some riders have tested positive and been punished, others have been allowed to get away with it.'

And his verdict on Armstrong, now serving his own life ban? 'My memory of him hasn't changed. I raced with him and that's it. It doesn't change what happened. What I lived with him, nobody can take that away.'

As for his own career, how does he reflect on it? With regrets? Pride? 'Sport is like life in general. Whatever has happened, there's bound to be things that you would want to change. But am I proud? Yes, I am. But there are things I would have changed in my normal life and in my sport. I would have changed my mentality, the way I approached cycling. It is a sport which absorbs you so much that everything bothers you and if I could go back in time, I'd want to change that. You don't know how to separate your personal life from your racing life, because you're living the sport twenty-four hours a day: training, diet, resting and on and on. So I would have been more with normal people, and enjoyed life more.

'Instead, when my racing was going badly, I was in a bad way with normal people and when my racing was going well, I'd be great with the rest of the world. But if it was bad, I'd be pissed off with everybody – my girlfriend, my family, my life. I had to separate my work from my personal life – that was it. That was what I needed to change. And now I look back and think, how stupid I was to be like that.'

Given that it had been so all-consuming, it must have been difficult to be cast out. Look at Pantani, or José María Jiménez, who also suffered from depression and died a few months before Pantani. Mayo snorts.

He heard the speculation that he might enter the kind of downward spiral that sucked in Pantani and Jiménez. 'To be honest, when I stopped I went through a difficult moment but I was surprised to hear about [the comparisons with] Pantani and all that,' Mayo says. 'I never thought about that.' On the contrary. 'The life I have now gives me a million opportunities. I'm really happy, not with the bike, but I've learned that life is very long. I'm enjoying things I never enjoyed before.'

He still rides. 'A little. I do some mountain biking, a bit more in the summer, and there's a cyclo-sportive event every year in Igorre, my village, which is in my name, and goes up the Urkiola climb, and I train for that. I play padel tennis, I go to the gym, see my clients and run my business and it's a good life. I'm not much in contact with cycling.'

Could he ever imagine working in cycling again? 'No.'

More food arrives – cheese and yet more cake. 'Yet more food arrives,' says Mayo, as though providing a running commentary. Then three bottles are plonked on the table: different varieties of Patxaran, the Basque liqueur. Mayo tells me I should taste all three.

'First I have one more question,' I tell him. 'You said when we met that cyclists were a bit crazy. Does that mean you think you're crazy too?'

'If you mean crazy in the sense of madness, no,' he says. 'And that's not what I meant. What I mean is it's

a crazy sport and if you're asking if the craziness of the
sport affected me, then yes.

'It's something that you can't escape. You're living
it twenty-four hours a day, and what you live, what
you eat, how you train, how you recover, everything
is important, every moment. It's a very selfish sport,
because it's a very individualistic sport, because it's up
to you to face up to responsibilities. And the craziness comes because of that: taking the sport and your
body, that degree of sacrifice, to extremes.

'I enjoyed it so much, but that's why I'm enjoying my normal life now,' Mayo continues. 'I can go
cycling but that era of professional cycling is over and
I can do what I want and I'm as happy as I've ever
been. Your point of view changes. And in fact, looking back, I sometimes end up surprised that I was a
cyclist at all.'

At this observation, he laughs: the laugh of
someone who did not have an ignominious end as
a cyclist, but a lucky escape, and a second chance.
Whatever he did in his cycling career, whatever he
was part of – and I would imagine that Mayo will
not be writing a tell-all book any time soon – he has
moved on so completely, cut his ties so comprehen-
sively, that he struggles to relate to the person, the
cyclist, he once was.

It's probably best that way. But it does make him
unusual.

And so it is that the fastest man ever to ride a bike up Mont Ventoux lives, happily, but so disconnected from the world of cycling that the rumour that he is a long-distance lorry driver can flourish. He is emblematic of an era, a product of a time and a region that pinned all its hopes on him. It seems especially poignant that we part as the sun sets and darkness falls, after two decades, on the Basque team, Euskaltel-Euskadi, for whom he dazzled so brightly, if briefly.

When we leave, Iban Mayo puts his orange puffa jacket back on and disappears into what is now night, walking along the footpath by the Nervión river, checking his phone, probably refreshing his Facebook page. The Scot is pissed now, but not in the way his friend meant.

Richard Moore is the author of six books, including *In Search of Robert Millar*, winner of Best Biography at the 2008 British Sports Book Awards, *Slaying the Badger*, and *Sunday Times* bestseller *Sky's the Limit*. His new book, *Étape*, which tells the untold stories of the Tour de France's defining stages, was published in June 2014.

9

Winning a stage race as part of a team is a tough-enough ask; trying to win one alone is another matter altogether.

Peter Cossins looks back at the career of Ken Russell, and celebrates one of Yorkshire's cycling heroes – one of many – with the tale of his attempt to win the 1952 Tour of Britain.

KEN RUSSELL'S TOUR

BY PETER COSSINS

Mention the name Ken Russell and for most people it will conjure up images of naked men wrestling in front of a blazing log fire or a huge white worm terrorising the Derbyshire countryside at the urging of a vampiric, blue-skinned Amanda Donohoe.

In Yorkshire, though, the name summons up a very different picture of one of Britain's most talented and yet unknown road racers, a rider so brilliant on his day that he won the Tour of Britain riding as a one-man team.

Born in the Bradford suburb of Idle in 1929, the two-wheeled Ken Russell was the youngest of three brothers.

'We lived in a back-to-back terrace, a one-up-one-down. The three of us boys slept in what we called the box room,' Russell recalls. 'My dad was a poorly man, really. He'd been in the First World War, and he'd got shell shock, and it had affected his mind. But he was a good man, and he started me off, really. He went around the rubbish tips and got me together a little bike – what they called a Ferris cycle at the time, with spoon brakes and solid tyres.'

Now eighty-four and living with Renee, his wife of more than sixty years, close to the quiet North Yorkshire town of Boroughbridge, he explains how his further introduction to cycling came, as it still does for so many from a poor background, from his daily ride to school. In his case, it was a sixteen-mile round trip with one of Bradford's many big hills to negotiate on the way.

'I suppose that's one of the things that got me really fit. I did that because I couldn't ride in the trolleybuses because I got travel sick.'

During the war years, Russell graduated to a bike that had been pieced together from parts lying around at what would become the famous Ellis Briggs shop/manufacturer in Shipley, on Bradford's northern edge.

'It was basically a touring bike built up from bits and pieces at Ellis Briggs, who weren't allowed to build bikes during the war because of the country's need for metal for the manufacture of weapons. My eldest brother worked there up until the point he volunteered for the RAF. He was in enamelling, I think. They did a fair bit of commercial enamelling, which was how they survived during the war, doing lots of re-enamelling of motorcycle frames, particularly for Scott Motorcycles.'

By now living in the Bradford suburb of Thackley, Russell joined a gang of friends on rides out to

popular cycling haunts such as York, Otley and
Knaresborough.

'I had a school friend in Thackley who was already
cycling fairly seriously, and he joined the Bradford
Racing Club, which was a league club, and he encouraged me to go and join them, and that was the start
of it, really,' says Russell. 'We'd go up into the Dales
to Buckden, over Fleet Moss, down to Hawes, over
Buttertubs, then over Birkdale Common to near
Kirkby Stephen, and then we'd cut back to Hawes and
over Fleet Moss and home. And it was all on a single
fixed gear.'

Although Russell only makes passing mention of
his club belonging to 'the league', his joining of a
club affiliated to the British League of Racing Cyclists
was a brave move. At that time, British cycling was
embroiled in what appears in hindsight to be the
most ridiculous of civil wars, which stemmed from
the authorities' desire to ban the use of bicycles on
the public highway. Although an amendment to the
Highways Act that would have brought this ban into
place was defeated in 1878, the attitudes that had
led to this amendment being proposed barely dissipated. Put simply, those in the governing classes were
unhappy at the prospect of working people roaming
the countryside freely on bicycles. The sport's ruling
body, the National Cyclists' Union (NCU), hardly
helped matters. At its AGM in 1888, a resolution was

passed discouraging road racing and banning all of its
officials from officiating at such events.

Although there were some dissenters, the ban
remained in place and unchallenged until 1942, when
Percy Stallard organised a massed-start event between
Llangollen and his hometown of Wolverhampton.
The NCU quickly banned all those who took part,
but Stallard's bold initiative quickly gathered support as new clubs emerged as members of the British
League of Racing Cyclists (BLRC). The league had
a particularly strong following in the West Midlands
and West Yorkshire, where Russell's Bradford club was
quick to take a lead in organising road-racing events.

The bad feeling between the rival organisations
continued for the best part of two decades, and ultimately cost Russell his racing career when he was still
very much in his prime. Sabotage of League races was
common, as Russell explains with an anecdote about
his own arrest during an event in 1948.

'It was just before I went into the Forces to do my
national service. It was the Nidderdale Road Race.
There were two events – a senior first-class event and
a junior race. We were in the first event, and when we
got to the crossroads at the Skipton–Harrogate road
at Killinghall, some police officers jumped out from
behind the pub there and stopped us. They started
taking names because we hadn't stopped at the "Halt"
sign. We didn't actually stop but if you put your foot

down it was supposed to be legal. It was a farce, really. Anyway, they booked us and summonsed us.

'I and another rider called Geoff Clark, who had ridden in that Llangollen–Wolverhampton race in 1942, decided we'd wait and warn the riders in the second event, which we did. While we were waiting, they were still at the side of the pub, and a private car came up to them filled with people in civvies. They were plainclothes policemen — it was like the Gestapo. They said, "We've got one and now we're waiting for the second event." They'd been tipped off by somebody. I don't know who it was for sure, but it was rather a coincidence that they were there.'

The riders arrested were summonsed to appear at the magistrates' court in Harrogate, by which point Russell was in the RAF and therefore unable to appear.

'We had a police sergeant in the club, and he said the best thing we could do was to get a solicitor and take it to court, which we did. The first thing the magistrate asked the police was, "Who did stop and who didn't stop?" They didn't have a clue because there were forty riders there, and they threw it out. They played hell with them for wasting police time.'

Russell admits he hadn't been looking forward to his national service, but ended up finding he had much more time for racing in uniform than he had previously.

'I rode all over the country, even in a race at the
Royal Albert Hall. It was a roller contest and the old
king and queen were there. It was part of the Festival
of Remembrance. Cycling in the Forces was in its
infancy, but started to take off at about that time. I
rode all over, mainly in time trials. I can always say
that every "fifty" and "hundred" I rode in, I won. I
only rode in one of each. When you look at the times
now they are laughable. It was four hours something
and they're way under four hours now,' he says.

After his year with the RAF, he returned to his job
with Whitaker and Mapplebeck, the Bradford-based
frame-builder.

'I was doing a bit of a frame-building, but mainly
mechanic-ing. Then they employed somebody and
we just didn't get on. He was an older chap and had
got a bit of an enlarged head, so I left and got a job
with Ellis Briggs. When I moved there I was building
frames in my own right, rather than helping someone
else as I had been before. I built the forks on my Tour
of Britain bike and I fettled the frame I raced on, but
I wanted the foreman at Ellis Briggs to build it for
the most part. It was the best bike I ever had, that,
without a doubt.'

Although the Tour de France had been founded
in 1903 and many other major races were established
on the continent around that time, it wasn't until
1951 that the inaugural Tour of Britain took place,

with substantial backing from the *Daily Express*. Russell rode it on a Whitaker and Mapplebeck bike as part of the ITP team, winning the stage into Wolverhampton, where his old mate Geoff Clark finished second. Yet he doesn't have fond memories of what was a ground-breaking race.

'What spoiled that first Tour of Britain for me was the organisation . . . The stage between Scarborough and Nottingham was a real mess. The race was supposed to turn left in Malton and go on from there to York. What I was told years after was that a police inspector in a car had come to the crossroads and ordered the policeman on duty there to "Get them straight through." He did just that and it caused the worst day's racing I've ever had.

'First of all, they said they would stop the breakaway and have a restart, but apparently the breakaway riders wouldn't stop. They eventually got them back on course and they stayed away all the way into Nottingham, but we were stopped again in York and told they were going to restart us, but they didn't. In the end, we were told to ride neutralised to Nottingham in the rain and cold, and by the time we got there I was suffering from hypothermia. I had to be lifted into the bath and couldn't start the penultimate stage the next day.'

Russell admits he can't remember who suggested that he ride in the second Tour of Britain, whether it was him or Ellis Briggs.

'It just seemed to happen,' he says. 'I didn't go in thinking about winning. I just thought I would do my best and see what happened, but I felt great for the whole fourteen days, and just had one or two incidents. One was on the stage from Glasgow to Dundee, where there was a breakaway and all of the top riders were in it except me. They were probably five minutes up or more. I got away myself and a Manchester lad came with me and we did bit-and-bit, and it were the best bit-and-bit I've ever had. We caught them going up into Perth. They were doing bit-and-bit and I dropped on to Bob Maitland's wheel. As he swung out to come through, he said to me: "Where the bloody hell have you come from?" He was one of the favourites, but never my favourite.

'The other one was from Nottingham to Norwich. We climbed a hill, not a long one, near Grantham. I realised I was boxed in. Whether they did it on purpose, I never knew, but there was a Sun rider and a BSA rider on my outside boxing me in. [Gordon] "Tiny" Thomas and a couple of others went off up the road, and I had to wait a few seconds before I could go off myself. I really did my nut, but I caught them in Grantham.'

Mention of his second place on the opening stage between Hastings and Southsea sends Russell off in search of a picture. He returns with a grainy image of the finish.

'Who won it?' he asks. It's clear that the rider on the left-hand side of the road has crossed the line first, the twenty-two-year-old Russell's dark curls and small, wiry frame marking him out as that man. 'That's right, it's me, but they gave it to the bloke in the middle [John Brackstone]. He's just ahead of the other two guys but he's nowhere near me.

'It was disputed at the time, but I never get involved with the judges,' says Russell, who did at least get the judges' verdict at another close finish in Blackpool a few days later. 'They had initially said Les Scales had won that one, but the riders themselves can tell best of all in a sprint finish. Les and I were good friends. It was close, but Les said to me: "I think you got that, Ken." I was sitting in the changing area at the Derby Baths in Blackpool with a few others and a chap came in and said, "They've changed it. They've given it to you."'

Russell then brings out a second image showing the finish in Blackpool.

'I got that picture from a still on Movietone news, which you can find on the Internet now,' he explains. 'Have a look and I guarantee that you'll laugh at it. Movietone just came up and pushed a microphone in front of me. They didn't say anything at all. I think I said, "Do you want me to speak?"'

Run in late August, the Tour of Britain was effectively a race linking most of the country's major resorts, which were all packed with holidaymakers. As a result, thousands turned out at stage starts and finishes.

'The crowds were tremendous and cycling's profile was pretty high,' Russell confirms. 'The *Daily Express* was covering it every day. If the *Daily Express* had continued sponsoring it, it would have grown and grown, but they got involved in this animosity between the League and the Union. I think that's why the *Daily Express* stopped doing it after 1954.'

Victory in the second stage from Southsea to Weymouth had given Russell the leader's yellow jersey. Bar two days when amateur Bill Bellamy claimed it – 'He was a real character and a super-stylish rider. When you looked at him, it looked like he was doing about twenty miles per hour, but he was actually doing about thirty' – Russell held it for the rest of the race, winning three stages in all along the way. Luck was with him as he only punctured twice, but he certainly deserved it as he had no teammates to rely on, while backup for his one-man team came from Ellis Briggs' 1936 long-bonnet Austin, which was so slow it was barely able to keep pace with the riders.

One of those punctures came on the very final day to Alexandra Palace in London, and provided what remains the most memorable episode of that race. Away at the front in a small group containing two rival BSA riders, with a third, Stan Jones, further ahead on his own, Russell realised he had a loose crank.

'That was no problem at all. I didn't think that it could have come off. It was a Sunlight cotterless. It had come loose, but it couldn't come off because there was a cap on it. That didn't bother me too much, but the puncture did. I felt it bottom-out, and fell back to Belgium's Marcel Michaux and asked him to have a look. He thought I was okay. We went on for probably a mile or two and it really bottomed hard, so I knew I had a puncture. Marcel and I had become a little bit friendly during the race, although not really close. He was a really good bloke. He was also the only one who could help me. I said to him: "*Donnez-moi votre bicyclette.*" He jumped off straight away and gave me it,' says Russell.

Such blatant collaboration between riders on different teams would be almost unthinkable now, but encapsulates the amateur ethos that still pervaded the sport at that time. It also led to a lifelong friendship between the Russell and Michaux families that continues today, even after Marcel Michaux's death.

'Marcel gave up his chance of the stage win, and he finished eighth overall as the best of the Belgians,' says Russell, who took the title by three minutes over runner-up Les Scales. He then confides: 'I've never told anybody this, but the Belgian team didn't like the fact he'd given me his bike because he got all of the publicity at the end. He actually presented the winner's trophy to me at the dinner in London.'

Russell returned to Bradford for a civic reception in front of the town hall. The main speaker was *Daily Express* sports editor Henry Rose, who was killed in the Munich air disaster six years later. Clearly more knowledgeable about football than cycling, he kept referring to Russell as 'Ken Sharples', despite shouts from the crowd.

Russell's prize for his remarkable one-man ride to Tour of Britain glory was £100, with a bit more for each of his stage wins, which gave him enough for a deposit on a house. He earned a fair degree of fame as well.

'I wasn't as much of a national figure as the big-name riders are today, but I suppose I was quite well known for a while. In fact, you can still see Ellis Briggs advertising my win on the Internet,' he says.

Asked what qualities made him such an impressive performer, Russell states: 'It might sound a bit big-headed, but I could sprint, I could climb and I could time trial pretty well.' The obvious follow-up question is why, having proved himself as the best road racer in Britain, he didn't turn his attention to racing on the Continent and the sport's biggest prizes. While believing he had the attributes required to do well abroad, Russell explains he remained in Bradford for three good reasons.

'By 1955, when I was still only twenty-six, I had a family and that meant me staying in Bradford. But

I also didn't want to go to Europe because even then I knew about the drug scene. I didn't want to get involved with that — no way! In my opinion, drugs almost ruined the sport. They were very near to ruining the Tour de France. After the death of Tommy Simpson, I can't believe that bike riders would want to carry on taking drugs.'

The final, almost ridiculous, reason was a ruling that decimated the top road-racing ranks in Great Britain. In 1954, the International Cycling Union instructed the BLRC to introduce fully professional races and do away with the 'independent' status that Russell and most other leading British riders had that enabled them to participate against both amateurs and professionals as well as each other. However, there were no races for professionals in the UK. The BLRC had expected amateur clubs to promote these events just as they had done semi-pro and amateur events in the past. But this never happened.

'I rode the BLRC Tour of Britain in 1955 and then received a letter saying they were discontinuing the independent class and they gave me a professional licence, but there were no professional races,' Russell confirms. 'I just threw it in the bin and that was it for me. Around that time a former clubmate came into the shop I was managing, and I said to him that I fancied building my own house. He wanted to do the same, so we got together and that were it. I packed up and built the house. That became our focus. I spent most of my working life with a firm called Yorkshire Heating, which is now a big company called Wolseley. I was a branch manager in Bradford for them for twelve good years.'

Russell devoted more time to cycling from the late 1980s, although not competitively. During those years he often rode with another Yorkshire great, Beryl Burton, particularly in the year or two before she died in 1996.

'The sad thing is that you see all these people making all this money today and I don't think she made very much at all. She was unfortunate, a bit like myself. We were born too soon.'

As I'm leaving, he goes off to find his copy of Chas Messenger's account of the history of the BLRC, *Ride and Be Damned*. He also suggests searching out the 1949 film *A Boy, a Girl and a Bike*.

'A lot of the people that I rode with appeared in it as extras, and it had some big names — Honor Blackman, Anthony Newley, Diana Dors, and even Jimmy Savile was in it, although they might want to cut him out now.'

Finally, one last question . . .

'The Tour's visit to Yorkshire? The first stage passes just a couple of miles away and I'll certainly be hoping to be out there to see it. It can do nothing but good, although I'm just a little bit worried about the narrow roads up in the Dales. They're not designed for that many riders.'

Few are better placed to offer that assessment than Ken Russell, one of Yorkshire's cycling greats.

Peter Cossins has written about professional cycling since 1993, is a contributing editor to *Procycling* magazine and is the editor of the *Official Tour de France Programme*. He is the author of *The Monuments: The Grit and the Glory of Cycling's Greatest One-Day Races* (Bloomsbury, March 2014) and has translated Christophe Bassons' autobiography *A Clean Break*, which is published by Bloomsbury on 3 July 2014.

10

Queen wanted to ride their bicycles where they liked, while Mark Ronson and friends want to ride theirs until they get home.

For centuries, music and cycling have gone hand-in-hand; a case, perhaps, of poetry in motion.

Ellis Bacon takes a closer look at some of the songs inspired by cycling, and finds that British bands the Delgados and Abdoujaparov share a love of bike racing almost as big as their namesakes.

TAPPING OUT A RHYTHM

BY ELLIS BACON

'*Bonjour, mon vieux.*'

Mark Ronson has just left some kind of game show, in some kind of Japanese metropolis, and uses some kind of watch to call in some kind of super-bike.

Just another day at the office for Ronson, no doubt.

In a *Power Rangers* meets *Knight Rider* meets *Transformers*-type sequence, a Raleigh Vektar-like bike appears after performing its own Brompton-style unfold (in fact, it really is a Brompton during the unfolding bits), and then makes some R2D2-like noises before it 'powers up' like KITT.

And after a quick costume change (and hair-colour) for Ronson, and a greeting for his bike in French, he's ready to roll.

Cue Spank Rock rapping into a payphone.

And oh! Here comes Kyle Falconer – the big-haired one-off of Scottish band The View – to have a bit of a sing about riding his bike until he gets home.

And here's Mark Ronson's wife, Joséphine de La Baume, and her achingly hip friends, on bikes, of course, to help Mark, Kyle and Spank foil a bike thief and then hang out in the sunny environs of east London – natch – looking like pretty much the coolest cycling club ever.

* * *

The bicycle in music goes way back. Thanks to 'The Bike Song', Ronson and his 'Business Intl' pals may well have assisted Wiggo, Cav, Vicky P and J Ken in making cycling as cool as it is these days, but they weren't the first to 'mash up' bikes 'n' songs. Oh no.

Harry Dacre's 'Daisy Bell' from 1892 is one of the oldest bike songs that people will have heard of – *Daisy, Daisy, give me your answer, do* . . . – with its bicycle built for two (because 'tandem' rhymes with nothing except 'memorandum') having to do the job as a wedding vehicle in place of a carriage, due to a lack of funds.

And even 'Daisy Bell' has been brought up to date – or up to the early '90s, at least – by having been raucously covered by Blur as a B-side to their single 'Sunday Sunday' from the album *Modern Life is Rubbish* in 1993.

So it would appear that bike-related songs are only the domain of the cool kids, and that was certainly the case in the '70s, although *everyone* was cool in the '70s.

Australian band The Mixtures' 'Pushbike Song'

– the black-and-white video for which shows the band pedalling around Melbourne on a range of bikes, including a penny farthing – was better known in the UK when it was covered by Mungo Jerry, whose version was slightly faster.

And in a nice piece of mutual back-scratching, the Mixtures covered what is arguably Mungo Jerry's best-known song, 'In the Summertime', which had nothing whatsoever to do with bikes, apart from being a good season during which to cycle.

Then there's possibly the greatest cycling song of them all.

Queen's 'Bicycle Race'? Close, but no guitar.

'Bike' by Pink Floyd (which also quickly descends into being nothing at all to do with a bike)?

Good effort, but no again . . .

Anyone who grew up in the '80s will suddenly remember it, and genuinely won't be able to stop singing it for about five weeks after their memory's been jogged: the 'Pedal Safety Song', as it was officially called – better known, perhaps, by the name of the Central Office of Information for the Department of Transport campaign it promoted: 'Get Yourself Seen'.

Okay, so it wasn't a 'chart hit'; rather, it was a road-safety advert for the – then – few people who dared ride a bike to school or work, full of tips about how not to be killed by a blind, drunk, or blind-drunk driver.

But it was camp and catchy, and is now retro-fantastic, so the powers that be could do a lot worse than re-run it, as it's ultimately a serious reminder to the cycling public to be careful, and to decrease their chances of being hit by using lights and wearing brightly coloured and/or reflective clothing.

At night, make it white,
In the dark, make it light –
But get yourself seen!
Take a brush to your bike,
Use some tape if you like –
But get yourself seen!

The best bit is when it ends (in two senses, perhaps), and a cheeky bike horn sounds. Find it on YouTube, and then wish you hadn't. But get yourself seen!

* * *

It's all very well writing a bike-related song, but tomorrow you might want to write a song about something else, like horse-riding, fishing, paint-balling, or doing anything for love.

Going one step further and actually naming your band after something cycling-related is going to stay with you that much longer.

Bombay Bicycle Club, from Crouch End in north London, don't count, because they're named after the chain of Indian restaurants. They're welcome to do a bike-related song if they like, though.

There's Campag Velocet – nearly named after the Campagnolo Veloce groupset – and then there are the big guns, brazenly naming themselves after real professional riders: Abdoujaparov and the Delgados. That's Abdoujaparov and, separately, the Delgados (although one, single super-band called 'Abdoujaparov and the Delgados' would be absolutely unbeatable in every respect).

Young Alun Woodward would become one of the lead singers of Scottish indie band the Delgados, but he had to come up with a name for the new group first.

'Like so many wee Scottish boys in the 1980s, I first saw cycling on Channel 4,' says Woodward. 'I'd been really into athletics before that – I used to run the 800 metres and the 1500 metres – but then I came in one day and saw the Tour de France on television for the first time, and was completely blown away by the drama of it all, and the beauty of people riding bikes up the sides of mountains.'

Woodward is from Motherwell, just outside Glasgow. 'So to see this Glaswegian guy winning the king of the mountains jersey totally personalised it for me,' he explains. 'The biggest thing for me with

Robert Millar was that at the time it wasn't that obvious how you got to the position he was in, in what
was quite an obscure sport, so there was more than a
touch of the maverick about him, which I was completely taken with.'

Woodward stopped running the day after he first
saw the Tour.

'It was all about cycling for me after that,' he says,
'and I was lucky with where I lived because there were
loads of great rides in and around the Clyde Valley.'

In 1994, Woodward and some friends got together
and formed a band. The other members weren't as
massively into cycling as him, but they were happy to
go with a cycling-related name.

'The two names it came down to choosing
between were the Delgados or Bernard Hinault,' says
Woodward – a simple choice between '88 Tour winner Pedro Delgado or five-time champion Hinault.

'Alternative or indie groups at the time were calling
themselves things like, I don't know, Teenage Fanclub,'
Woodward says, name-checking the fellow Scottish
band. 'Bands weren't really calling themselves "The"-
something – that was more popular in the '60s and '70s.'

Nevertheless, or perhaps because of that, they
decided to go for the Delgados.

'I liked Delgado,' Woodward says. 'He was such an
amazing, explosive rider, but there was also that year
[1986] when he pulled out of the Tour because his

mother had died, which was really touching.'

The Delgados' first album, in 1996, was called *Domestiques*, followed by *Peloton* in 1998. None of the songs were ever anything to do with cycling, though.

'I guess we just all had different interests,' says Woodward, 'but we got to a point with the album titles where we just thought it was getting stupid, and decided to call the next one something completely different.'

That third album – *The Great Eastern* – was nominated for the Mercury Prize in 2000.

The band split in 2005, and Woodward went on to perform solo as Lord Cut-Glass, while he and the rest of the Delgados are all still involved in the running of their own record label, Chemikal Underground, in Glasgow.

Chemikal Underground also released Mogwai's first two albums, in 1997 and 1999, and we chat briefly about Mogwai's soundtrack to *Zidane: A 21st Century Portrait* – a French documentary film that focuses entirely on footballer Zinedine Zidane during a single match.

'Oh, and another thing is that there's a documentary being made about Graeme Obree, and I'm writing the music for that, actually,' Woodward adds, as though it's no big deal. 'Talking about the Mogwai film just reminded me.'

He's not allowed to say much more, and isn't sure

when it's due out, but he's written some of the music for it already, he says, and is now looking forward to seeing the footage of Obree's attempt in 2013 at the human-powered world speed record in Nevada.

It will be a documentary well worth watching, following hot on the heels of the Marco Pantani film, *Pantani: The Accidental Death of a Cyclist*, released in 2014, and you'll be able to impress your now-interested-in-cycling mates at the pub with your knowledge that the original soundtrack was composed by one of the lead singers of the Delgados, who – did you know? – were named after 1988 Tour de France winner Pedro Delgado.

* * *

Abdoujaparov is a punk band led and founded by Carter USM's Les 'Fruitbat' Carter. The inspiration for the name came from the Uzbek sprinter Djamolidine Abdoujaparov, of course.

'It was around the time when we were recording the Carter USM EP *A World Without Dave*,' explains Carter. 'The '96 Tour de France was on at the time, and when Abdoujaparov won that mountain stage [stage 14, between Besse and Tulle], I remember turning around and saying to Jim [Morrison – but not *that* one], "If I ever have another band, I'm going to call it Abdoujaparov." It was one of those names that took you a while to get right when you were learning cyclists' names, wasn't it? I thought it would be such a brilliant name for a band, because no one would be able to pronounce it, so it was deliberately chosen for that reason.'

When, in 1998, Carter USM split up (for the first time), Carter did start his own band – and called it Abdoujaparov.

'Every time I meet new people and tell them the name, they say, "Abdouboudouba . . . Abadoudou . . . What!? That's just a collection of letters! That's not a name!"' he laughs. Mission accomplished.

Carter used to be a very keen cyclist himself.

'I used to time trial, very badly, back in the day. I belonged to the Dulwich Paragon CC for a while,' he says. 'I was working as a cycle courier, which got me to a level of fitness where I could actually do something on the bike, but to be honest my time-trial results weren't that great!'

Carter's still got his Geoffrey Butler – 'it's got Reynolds 531 tubing, and is almost vintage now!' – and rides it around where he lives in Folkestone.

'I can't cycle that much any more, because I've buggered my back and my knee, so long distances are out, which is what I used to like doing,' he explains. 'I just pootle around a bit, but it's massively hilly everywhere around here, and that really does my knee.'

He says that there are apparently quite a few fans of cycling in the music business, and a couple spring to mind.

'Mike [Edwards] from Jesus Jones is a massive cyclist, as is Mary Byker, from Pop Will Eat Itself. They're still into their cycling quite a lot, those two,' he says. 'They're the main ones I can remember, because they were always trying to make me go out on rides with them.'

Fronting his own band in Abdoujaparov meant that Carter could incorporate his passion for cycling into some of the songs' lyrics. 'The Abdoujaparov Theme', for example, is all about the rider from whom the band got its name.

He's a dangerous man from Uzbekistan.
He is 'The Tashkent Terror' and I can't say fairer.
And he don't give a fuck, coz he took too many drugs
*   (allegedly).*
And I love him very much, we try to keep in touch.

'But there's also a song called "Fish Face",' says Carter, 'which is about riding in London, from the perspective of a cyclist, basically swearing at people that try to kill them.'

I don't suppose you have ever read The Highway Code.
You know that you shouldn't be allowed on the road.
I remember when the bicycle was safe and it was fun.
The next time I cycle I'm gonna bring a gun!

'That one always goes down well with the cyclists I know,' he laughs.

As Fruitbat, Carter also had quite a penchant for cotton cycling caps, and would wear them while performing with Carter USM.

'I was really into cycling, and was beginning to go a little bit bald on top, so I thought, "Hat!"' he explains, and says that he's still got a massive collection of them somewhere in his garage.

'Although, actually, I had to throw quite a lot of them away because the cat pissed on them, unfortunately.'

As for how he got to have so many of them in the first place, it's not that he simply spent all his hard-earned cash from being in Carter USM on them.

'It used to be on our band rider that there had to be three cycling caps at each gig we did,' Carter laughs. 'People were really panicking, trying to find them, at some places, so that was quite fun. They were nearly always there, though!'

Did he have a favourite?

'I used to have a Jolly hat that I really liked, and I think there was one of the early Lotto ones that I wore quite a lot, too.'

Look hard, and the cycling cap can be found in various examples of popular culture: Wesley Snipes wears both a Colnago and a Time cap in the basketball film *White Men Can't Jump*, while Mariah Carey goes for a Vitalicio Seguros one – really quite randomly – for her 2001 film *Glitter*.

Big names, but Fruitbat wore one best, plumping for a light-blue Z cap – Z was Greg LeMond, Robert Millar and Ronan Pensec's team in the '90s – for Carter USM's infamous televised performance at the *Smash Hits* Poll Winners Party in 1991. But first, a word of warning: Phillip Schofield fans – look away now.

The band played 'After the Watershed', and then smashed up the stage, in time-honoured fashion.

'Blimey! That was original!' quipped host Schofield, and then let out a tiny whimper as he was rugby-tackled from out of nowhere by Fruitbat, and the crowd went mad.

'I was absolutely furious,' says Carter. 'I mean, poor Phil – he didn't know what he was getting into, did he?'

Search for something along the lines of 'smash hits carter' and you'll find four minutes of entertaining YouTube footage.

As Carter and Morrison left the building, they were told that they'd never be on television again.

'But that was rubbish; we were back on telly a week later.'

Carter says that it was an unfortunate episode in that the rugby-tackling-Phillip-Schofield thing ended up being one of the things that the band is best remembered for, rather than the music.

'And that's a bit depressing sometimes,' Carter says. 'I've actually just done yet another of those things for the telly, in which they look back at stuff that's happened, like that. It was the fifth time I've done one of those, and I've just decided that I'm not going to do it again.'

Carter says he's not seen Schofield since, but that a few messages were passed back and forth between them in the aftermath.

'Not really apologies, but . . . Well, he did all right for himself after that. He's on telly being very respected and grey-haired now, isn't he?'

Carter USM (USM stands for 'The Unstoppable Sex Machine') will play their final-ever gig at the Brixton Academy in November 2014.

'One of the reasons we kept getting back together was because we found that we were kind of being dismissed from the history of pop,' says Carter. 'Whenever you have one of those things looking back at the '90s, we never get a mention. We were being erased from history, even though we headlined Glastonbury. But you watch something about the '90s and it's all about Oasis, Blur, and the whole Britpop thing.'

But he and lead singer Jim Bob – a novelist and solo artist today – proved what they set out to do, which was, says Carter, to be able to consistently sell out the Brixton Academy if they wanted to.

It may soon be the end for Carter USM, but

Abdoujaparov are still going strong, keeping the now-retired dangerous man from Uzbekistan's name alive.

PLAYLIST*

'Pushbike Song' – The Mixtures

'The Abdou Theme' – Abdoujaparov

'Machineries of Joy' – British Sea Power

'Daisy Bell' – Blur

'The Bike Song' – Mark Ronson and the
    Business Intl

'Bicycle Race' – Queen

'To Lose La Trek' – Campag Velocet

'Bike' – Pink Floyd

'Pedal Safety Song' [aka 'Get Yourself Seen']
    – Central Office of Information for the
    Department of Transport

'Fish Face' – Abdoujaparov

Please listen responsibly – i.e. not while riding

Ellis Bacon contributes to various cycling magazines, including *Cycle Sport*, *Cycling Weekly* and *Cyclist*. He is the author of *World's Ultimate Cycling Races* and *Mapping Le Tour* (both Collins), and translated Bjarne Riis's autobiography, *Riis: Stages of Light and Dark* (Vision Sports Publishing).

11

History is usually written by the victor and Stephen Roche's account of his 1987 Tour de France victory is well known.

But what about the man Roche defeated in that incredible, topsy-turvy Tour?

Alasdair Fotheringham travelled to Madrid to meet Pedro Delgado to get his side of the story.

All the focus was on the fact that Roche became Ireland's first Tour champion but Delgado was bidding to become only the third Spaniard to win the race, an achievement that had to be postponed by a year.

THE OTHER SIDE OF THE COIN

BY ALASDAIR FOTHERINGHAM

I'm standing at a crossroads in the centre of Madrid, counting the minutes as they tick past our meeting time when I remember the cliché about Pedro Delgado. He is always late. In fairness, this reputation owes much to one incident at the *Grand Départ* of the 1989 Tour de France in Luxembourg when, as defending champion, he turned up almost three minutes late for his allotted start time for the prologue time trial.

Just as I'm about to check the time again, he arrives. Now aged fifty-three, he still looks as fit as a fiddle, a little greyer around the temples perhaps, and he's apologetic for the delay.

I'm here to talk to Delgado not about his time-keeping or about the Tour de France he won in 1988 but the one he lost to Stephen Roche the year before.

* * *

The 1987 Tour is memorable for a number of reasons. The start was in West Berlin, symbolising the beginning of the Tour's expansion from a rather more parochial French event into a fully international race.

The organisers were embracing teams and riders from all over the globe. In 1983, a team of Colombians had been invited to take part, now they had two squads – Café de Colombia and Ryalcao-Postobon – and the Colombian contingent numbered twenty riders.

The Tour, once dominated by a handful of nations, was now a platform for diversity and this melting pot of cultures was demonstrated no more graphically then when photographers asked Colombia's leading rider Luis Herrera, nicknamed Lucho, to pose next to the Berlin Wall. It would be another couple of years before Eastern Europe, and the countries behind the Iron Curtain, would be welcomed fully into the Tour family, although there were a few notable exceptions. Poland's Lech Piasecki took the yellow jersey in West Berlin and the British ANC-Halfords squad included Kvetoslav Palov, who was born in Czechoslovakia. The American 7-Eleven squad returned, having made their debut the previous year, and the British ANC-Halfords team were handed an invite partly, one suspects, as a way to mark the twentieth anniversary of Tom Simpson's death on Mont Ventoux.

And it was on Mont Ventoux that Jean-François Bernard staked his claim to the throne recently abdicated by Bernard Hinault, the five-time Tour champion who had retired at the end of the previous season, a little prematurely perhaps, at the age of thirty-two. Bernard won the time trial there, taking the yellow jersey, albeit briefly.

But for Irish cycling, the race is iconic for Roche's victory and particularly for his pivotal performance at La Plagne in the Alps, where he limited his losses to Delgado when it looked as if the Spaniard was poised to win. It was one of the Tour's most dramatic days. Delgado made his move for overall victory, believing he had to extend his lead over Roche before the time trial in Dijon. Roche, seemingly exhausted, held the gap at a manageable distance before digging deep in the closing kilometres and appearing round the final bend just as Delgado was crossing the line.

Phil Liggett, commentating for British television, uttered the famous line: 'That looks like Roche. That looks like Stephen Roche! It's Stephen Roche!'

Delgado had gained time on the Irishman, but only four seconds, which he knew was nowhere near enough.

Exhausted, Roche collapsed to the ground and was given oxygen by the medics but it was Delgado's Tour ambitions that needed reviving.

At the time, Roche's victory was the second closest in Tour history. His margin was just forty seconds. Delgado had not just run him close, there were several points in the race when it looked like he had done enough, only to find Roche a persistent foe. Delgado dropped Roche at Villard-de-Lans, then took the yellow jersey from him at Alpe d'Huez, holding it through the Alps but failing to open an unassailable lead. Roche, comfortably the better time triallist, overturned Delgado's lead in Dijon.

Roche's version of events is well known. History is written by the victor, so they say, but often it is the other side of the coin that puts events into perspective. I wanted to hear Delgado's story and so that was why I found myself waiting for him on a Madrid crossroads on a cold, crisp winter's day.

As we begin to talk, it's clear there's no hint of bitterness in him, perhaps because he did win the Tour the following year.

Delgado made his Tour debut in 1983 and was lying second overall, just over a minute behind Laurent Fignon, when he got an upset stomach and had to pull out of the race. The following year, he was fourth overall and well in contention for the king of the mountains prize when he crashed into a concrete post on the descent of the Joux-Plane, fracturing his collarbone. In 1985, he finished sixth overall and won the mountain stage at Luz Ardiden in the Pyrenees. Then, in 1986, he was in fifth place overall when his mother died and he pulled out of the race.

Delgado had won the Vuelta a España in 1985, though, when Spanish interests aligned to prise the yellow jersey from the slender shoulders of Scotland's Robert Millar on the penultimate day.

By the summer of 1987, the Tour had entered something of a power vacuum. Hinault's retirement had left the race without its figurehead, its *patron*, and there was no one ready to assume the position. Greg LeMond, the defending champion, was recovering from a near-fatal shooting accident he'd suffered while on a turkey-hunting trip in the spring. Roche had been third overall in 1985, behind Hinault and LeMond, and had endured a terrible Tour in 1986 before winning the Giro d'Italia less than a month before the start in West Berlin. Few thought he could repeat the act so soon.

Of the rest, there was the mercurial Urs Zimmermann of Switzerland, a fine climber and third overall in 1986 but not thought to be robust enough to win; Ireland's Sean Kelly, who had a string of high finishes to his name but was vulnerable in the heat and the big mountains; Andy Hampsten of the United States was talented but callow. That left Delgado; the Colombians Luis Herrera and Fabio Parra and a French trio of Laurent Fignon, champion in 1983 and 1984 but as likely to abandon as he was win, Charly Mottet and Jean-François Bernard in a long list of candidates. There were plenty of pretenders but no outright favourite.

'I went to the Tour with a simple question in my head,' says Delgado. 'What on earth was going to happen? Every year since 1983, when I had almost taken the lead at one point, something had gone badly wrong for me. I had no idea if 1987 was going to be different. To be honest, before the start, I thought the Tour was cursed for me.'

Delgado was in his second season with the Dutch PDM team. Despite knowing his contract was to expire at the end of the year, he did not have much interest in renewing for a third.

Results at PDM had been fairly low-key – his stage win at the 1986 Tour and fourth place in the 1987 Vuelta were about all he had to show. At the time, Dutch teams had a reputation for being insular too. 'The Dutch riders weren't very interested in supporting me,' he says. 'The sports director, Jan Gisbers, was okay. I got on well with him but I never had their real backing. I was the leader but only on paper. I only really got on well with Adri van der Poel.'

Early on in the Tour, the team management told Delgado that LeMond would be joining PDM at the start of 1988. 'PDM wanted me to stay but what was the point if LeMond could get a minute-and-a-half on me in the time trials? If I attacked in the mountains I'd be accused of disloyalty.' LeMond's arrival would either straitjacket Delgado or force him to do the legwork for his teammate. 'I told PDM I was quitting and as soon as I did that I had all the Spanish teams – Reynolds, BH and Kelme – calling me,' says Delgado.

Knowing his departure was inevitable, it was perhaps not surprising that PDM's riders did not put their backs into helping Delgado. He had one loyal teammate, a Spaniard called José Luis Laguia, who had won the king of the mountains title at the Vuelta a record five times. But Rooks and Theunisse were not much help. 'I sincerely believe they told Rooks to race for himself and whoever was ahead overall was the team leader,' says Delgado.

In the absence of team support, Delgado chose to look after himself during the first week, racing the way Spanish riders are brought up to race. Towards the end of stage three to Stuttgart, there was a little climb. Delgado chose the moment to attack and he gained ten seconds. 'It was all part of the classic Spanish philosophy of gaining as much time as possible before the time trials mess things up for you,' he says.

Many of the English-speaking riders, particularly those from the ANC-Halfords team who were thrown into the Tour and asked to sink or swim, recall a fiercely hot, fiercely fast opening week, but Delgado does not remember it that way. 'The worst for me was 1983, my first. It was hard in 1987, for sure, but it doesn't stick out in the memory as being that bad.'

The lack of an outstanding favourite made for an open race and the yellow jersey passed from rider to rider in the first half. Prologue winner Jelle Nijdam to Piasecki, then Roche's Carrera teammate Erich

Maechler and then two Système-U riders, Charly Mottet and Martial Gayant, all held the lead.

Although Roche won the incredibly long 87.5-kilometre time trial from Saumur to Futuroscope, Delgado still did not consider the Irishman a major threat. Instead, he feared the Colombians, and particularly Herrera, who had won the Vuelta a España in the spring. 'They had ripped that Vuelta apart, even when it was freezing cold in Andorra, and I thought they would do the same again at the Tour. My real worries were the Colombians, Fignon, Bernard and Mottet.'

Mottet, in particular, was a dangerous man once he took the yellow jersey after the Futuroscope time trial, even if *L'Équipe*'s assertion that he was the next Tour winner seemed a little premature.

'I was focusing very hard on myself,' says Delgado. 'After the Futuroscope time trial, I started to feel I could do a good Tour. It was the longest time trial I had ever done – by a long way – and I was tenth. I thought I was a poor time triallist and feared it could only go badly but it was actually pretty good.'

Giuseppe Saronni, who had won the Giro d'Italia in 1979 and 1983, was the rider who set out two minutes before Delgado that day. Around halfway into his race, he saw Saronni and shortly he caught and passed him. 'I had been riding pretty calmly in the first half of the time trial because I was worried about falling apart on such a long course.' Inspired by passing the

Italian, Delgado pushed harder in the second half and finished strongly. 'It was a different story in the second half.' He finished tenth, moving up to fifteenth overall, 3mins18secs down on Roche but with the mountains of the Pyrenees and Alps, his prime hunting ground, still to come. The time trial also sorted out the pecking order in the PDM team. His teammates may not have been any more inclined to work for him but he was now their definitive leader.

Delgado was invigorated by his time trial result and the next day he started to chip away at those ahead of him, taking seventeen seconds on the rolling stage to Chaumeil. The time trial had taken its toll on many, but not Delgado, and he was further encouraged by the fact that none of the teams were able to control the race, not even the French Système-U squad, which had Mottet in the yellow jersey and Fignon well placed. As soon as the Pyrenees arrived, Delgado moved up by default as the climbers all moved up the general classification as the roads steepened. He jumped from fifteenth to sixth and was suddenly one of the main players.

* * *

But it turned out that Delgado's big mistakes were to overestimate the threat posed by the Colombians and underestimate Roche. 'He was a smart guy, a good wheel to follow because he always seemed to be in the right place at the right time, but I had seen him blow badly in the heat during the 1986 Tour. That was why I never thought he'd be a Tour winner. I didn't see him as a great rival until it was too late.'

In turn, Roche was also worried about Herrera and the Frenchman Jean-François Bernard, who gained more than three-and-a-half minutes at the end of the Pyrenean stage to Pau, which crossed the Col du Soudet and Col de Marie-Blanque.

If Delgado considered the threat posed by the Colombians as a collective effort, that's because it was. Although there were two rival teams, and a couple of Colombians in European teams, they operated as a unit. 'They were like a little army,' he says. Herrera and Fabio Parra, a former economics student, of the Café de Colombia team were the most dangerous. 'Herrera had all the class and Parra was constantly making clever, calculated attacks,' says Delgado. 'I based my race around them. I knew that if I stuck with them in the mountains I'd pan them in the time trials.'

The stage to Luz Ardiden was even more impor- tant. The Norwegian Dag-Otto Lauritzen won, although he was no concern overall, and Delgado was far more interested in the fortunes of the riders around him in the standings. Roche lost six seconds to Delgado, Bernard conceded almost a minute and a half and Mottet lost two minutes of his advantage, although he kept hold of the yellow jersey. Herrera gained almost ninety seconds on Delgado as he continued to claw back time. Although almost eight minutes down, at the rate he was recovering his losses, Herrera was bound to be a factor in the final week. On the other hand, Roche's performance still didn't cause alarm. Roche was still third overall but Delgado felt he was living on borrowed time and would surely fall back in the Alps. Delgado was now fourth, perfectly poised to strike.

There was a torrential rainstorm during stage 15 as the race exited the Pyrenees. It was supposed to be a routine stage but Roche lost almost a minute after deciding to drop back to his team car to get a rain jacket. It is indicative of Delgado's lack of preoccupation with Roche that he does not remember that at all. He was still fixated on the Colombians and was impressed that Herrera had managed to stay in the front group in such awful conditions.

* * *

The time trial at Mont Ventoux was one of the most important tests of the Tour. It was a day when Jean-François Bernard staked his claim to the yellow jersey. 'Bernard was supposed to be the new Hinault. He raced on Hinault's old team,' says Delgado. 'He was young, he was an outsider and had a lot of potential. The Ventoux was Bernard's crowning moment. He did everything right, using a special time-trial bike on the ten or twelve kilometres on the flat to the foot of the climb and then a lightweight road bike on the climb itself. He panned us.'

Bernard defeated Herrera by one minute 39 seconds, with Delgado third, almost two minutes slower, and Roche a further twenty-eight seconds back. Bernard took the yellow jersey and the manner of his performance made him the new favourite, but really the Tour was now down to those four and Mottet, who was still third.

Delgado's result was even more impressive because he had never ridden Mont Ventoux before. 'That was the first time I had ever gone up it. I had no reference points whatsoever, but it was like when I finished second at the Puy de Dôme during my first Tour. Even though I had no idea what I was facing, if you're in good shape it doesn't matter if you know a climb, you do the best you can.

'Either way, I was really pleased with what happened. I still worried that the Colombians, who were still a long way off overall, would blow the race apart in the Alps.'

The 19th stage from Valréas to Villard-de-Lans was the sort of anarchic day Delgado contends does not happen any more. 'That was one of those great cycling moments,' he says. A combination of factors led to a significant reshuffle of the general classification. 'It was one of those days where you had a star like Fignon who had a general attitude towards racing of anything goes. If you fell off, or punctured, it was a case of "See you at the finish!"'

Laurent Fignon, Mottet's Système-U teammate helped cause havoc, attacking through a feed zone on the approach to the Col de la Chau. The problem was, Bernard, the *maillot jaune*, had punctured, waited a long time to get a replacement wheel and was still making his way back up to the group of favourites.

'Hot-spot sprints and feed zones were a real danger. At the feed zone, which was at the foot of a climb – not a very hard climb but very long – Système-U went absolutely ballistic. It was pretty chaotic – feed stations always were. They say Bernard was at the back when he picked up his feedbag because he had punctured before that. Fignon really went for it and I think that Bernard relaxed a bit too much. Either way, before Bernard knew it, a group of twenty had a minute's lead and he had to chase.' All the other favourites were there and the Tour's general classification was being reshuffled without Bernard.

Towards the top of the Côte de Chalimont, a first-category climb, Delgado attacked and Roche went with him. Delgado knew that if they worked together, Roche would take the yellow jersey but he was not overly concerned because there were still three very difficult mountain stages – Alpe d'Huez, La Plagne and Morzine – to go. There would be plenty of opportunity to eliminate Roche before the time trial and Delgado preferred to go head-to-head with Roche than allow Mottet, Bernard or Herrera to stay in contention. So he set the pace, knowing he was making important gains.

'I didn't care that I was doing most of the work. I thought I was eliminating a lot of rivals, particularly the Colombians, and I thought Roche would self-destruct in the Alps. I thought I had won the Tour.

'But I lacked ambition. When we got to Villard-de-Lans, there was a slight uphill and I gave it everything with five hundred metres to go. I turned round and couldn't believe Roche wasn't there. He was really on the limit that day.'

Had he realised that, he would have attacked earlier and gained more time on Roche than the three seconds he did take. Delgado was now third, one minute and nineteen seconds behind Roche, with Mottet sandwiched between them.

Delgado's attitude is understandable. He was exhilarated, having ruled Herrera and Bernard out of the picture. The Frenchman lost 4mins16secs and any chance of winning the Tour.

Suddenly, instead of fearing another bout of misfortune, Delgado began to spot omens. His race

number was 51, said to be lucky, and worn by the
likes of Eddy Merckx, Luis Ocaña and Bernard
Thévenet when they won the Tour. In the entire history of the race, only two Spaniards had won before:
Federico Bahamontes in 1959 and Ocaña fourteen
years later, in 1973. Fourteen years had elapsed since
Ocaña's victory. It felt destined to be.

At Alpe d'Huez, Roche suffered a mini collapse,
just as Delgado had anticipated. Another Spaniard,
Federico Echave won the stage, Delgado was seventh
and Roche was one minute and 44 seconds behind
him. Delgado was in yellow for the first time.

'It was hot and Mottet cracked completely. My idea
had been to drop Roche on the climb of Alpe d'Huez,
or follow the Colombians when they attacked, as they
always did, then strike out on my own if possible.
Roche was twenty-five seconds behind me overall but
there was still La Plagne to come.'

Delgado estimated that he needed a lead of ninety
seconds over Roche going into the time trial at Dijon.
'I was over the moon on Alpe d'Huez and thought the
Tour was mine,' he says. Even Roche admitted he felt
the advantage lay with Delgado. Either way, the fans
were enjoying a slugfest that was a little like a boxing
match. Roche was on the ropes but he was handling
everything Delgado could throw at him and was not
on the canvas yet.

On the stage to La Plagne, Roche, the great bluffer,

attacked at the foot of the penultimate climb, the Col de la Madeleine. It was the last thing Delgado expected, and at first he didn't even know Roche had escaped. 'I knew that Theunisse, my teammate, was away, which suited me, but when I heard Roche was up there, we took it steady, hoping he would burn himself out before the top. It's twenty kilometres long and sure enough, we reached him before the summit.'

On the valley road towards La Plagne, Delgado discussed possible tactics with the Colombians. Where once he had feared their explosive attacks, now he could use them as a foil. Seeking allies to make the climb as uncomfortable as possible to Roche, Delgado hoped to join forces. 'But they weren't interested, so I went for it alone. And for most of the climb, it went perfectly.'

Delgado kept getting updates on the time gap from his team car. It stayed steady at a minute. 'This was all right, even if I'd have liked a bit more, because it gave me the ninety seconds I wanted overall. But then Lucho [Herrera] came up to me and passed me and finally, in the last three kilometres, I suddenly cracked completely.'

Delgado was done for. A combination of four days of hard racing and the pressure of having the yellow jersey sunk him. 'There was fog at the top of La Plagne and I was totally exhausted so the last two kilometres felt like they were never-ending. I was starting to worry Roche would overtake me. All I could think of as a way to keep my morale up was to think that if I was suffering badly, he must be feeling even worse. Well, imagine how bad I felt when I found out he'd done so well.'

Roche had been playing a patient game. He kept Delgado's advantage as steady as possible and decided to save what energy he had for an all-or-nothing assault on the final couple of kilometres.

As Delgado hit the line, the hunched figure of Roche appeared in the finishing straight. 'They told me it was only four seconds' difference and my world fell apart.'

Roche was later penalised ten seconds for an illegal feed – taking food in the final twenty kilometres, which is against the rules. But even with that, Delgado's overall lead was only thirty-nine seconds, nowhere near the minute-and-a-half he felt he needed as a buffer in the time trial.

* * *

Delgado admits he did not think Roche could do so well on the long climbs. 'I thought he was someone who could hang on on the ten-kilometre climbs but that anything over that would be too much,' he says. At Morzine, Roche struck another blow to Delgado's morale by attacking him on the notoriously dangerous descent of the Joux-Plane, gaining another eighteen seconds. 'I had tried to drop him on the climb of the Joux-Plane but my head had fallen off after La Plagne,' he says. 'I'd given it everything but it hadn't worked. My plan of being ninety seconds ahead for the time trial was down the pan. I hurt him a bit on the Joux-Plane but I couldn't shake him. After La Plagne, my heart wasn't in it.'

In his mind, the Tour was lost. In the rolling thirty-eight-kilometre time trial Roche, an excellent *rouleur*, would easily overturn Delgado's slender advantage to win the Tour.

'Had I been a bit more experienced, things could have been different, but I've never done a time trial as badly as I did that one. I was feeling so tense and I was sure I'd already lost.

'I wasn't great at time trials anyway. I'd grown up in Spanish teams and they wouldn't let you have a time-trial bike until the day of the race. Rather than let you get used to it, and adapt to it, on the morning of the time trial they would give you the bike and say "Here's a bike you can go fast on."'

Delgado was also wary of the new technology that had revolutionised the time-trial bikes in the mid-1980s. He was scarred after using disc wheels during the 1985 Tour. 'I was going at eighty-five kilometres an hour through a wood when there was a clearing and a gust of wind carried me from one side of the road right to the edge of the other. I never even knew how I ended up there. It was a miracle I wasn't killed . . . a real arse-clencher.'

The Dutch PDM team were light years ahead of the Spaniards when it came to embracing the technological advances available but Delgado is blunt when he says: 'I viewed technology as a nightmare.'

In fact, Delgado had to 'lose' the Tour before he settled into any kind of rhythm. 'Maybe if I'd been a bit more mature, I'd have given him a fright. In the third week of a grand tour, nobody has much advantage in terms of technique. You win or lose on brute strength,' he says. 'I wasn't totally exhausted, in fact I'd recovered a bit from the mountains during the flat stage the day before, but I went into the time trial so nervous, so demoralised because I couldn't handle the pressure. The more nervous I got, the more angry I got with myself and that made it worse.'

So the Tour slipped away. Delgado led Roche by twenty-one seconds going into the time trial and trailed by forty seconds afterwards.

'With the benefit of hindsight, you look back and realise your mistakes, like at Villard-de-Lans,' says Delgado of the day when he perhaps had the opportunity to turn the screw on Roche. 'I wasn't angry with myself because I realised that sometimes the race played out in my favour, like when Fignon blew the race apart, and at other points it didn't. People say I ought to have won the race but I don't agree. I could have, perhaps, if the cards had fallen a bit differently, but that's a very different thing.'

After the time trial, Delgado congratulated Roche. There was no ill-feeling between them despite the fact they'd fought so doggedly on the bike. 'Roche deserved to win it. There was one school of thought at the time – the Fignon school of thought, as I called it – that if a rider was your enemy [in the race], he was your enemy twenty-four hours a day. I didn't believe that. In fact, I got a huge bollocking in the Spanish media for giving Roche a *bidon* [a water bottle] during one of the stages. My attitude was that if I was thirsty, he would do the same. At least I *think* he would have. Either way, it was a good race. From Futuroscope onwards there wasn't a dull day.'

At the end of the year, he left PDM, joining the Spanish Reynolds team. His replacement, LeMond, took longer than expected to recover from his gunshot injury and barely raced for them, moving on to the small Belgian ADR team after just one year. With them, LeMond won the 1989 Tour.

In the meantime, Delgado won the 1988 Tour for Reynolds, comfortably defeating PDM's Steven Rooks, who was runner-up. That, he says, was thanks to his defeat in the previous year's race. He knew he was not cursed in July. 'At the very least, I knew that the Tour was not something where I would

automatically do badly. I got the feeling back that
I had had in 1983, at my first Tour, that one day I
would win it.'

Alasdair Fotheringham is the Spanish correspondent and
cycling specialist for the *Independent* and the *Independent on
Sunday*. He is the author of *Reckless* (Bloomsbury, 2014), a
biography of the 1973 Tour de France winner Luis Ocaña.

12

The question will be all-too-familiar
to professional riders past and present:
'Have you ridden the Tour de France?'

Tom Southam is one of those who
never did ride the world's biggest race
during his career. But through his own
experiences, and through interviews
with fellow riders in the same boat, he
discovers that the Tour perhaps isn't the
be-all-and-end-all after all.

THE NEARLY MEN

BY TOM SOUTHAM

Sometime in July of 2005, I found myself sitting outside a quaint English pub on a summer's afternoon, drinking cider and listening to the sounds of a game of club cricket being played on a nearby village green. I was in Hayfield in the Peak District, and I was there in the company of (a then mid-suspension) David Millar.

With both of us having spent more years than we cared to remember outside of the UK, adapting to life on the continent in order to make a living in the sport we loved, we were having quite a rare afternoon enjoying the idyllic and quintessentially British setting. For a while, the world of European professional bike racing that we both lived in couldn't have seemed further away.

But, while I would have been happy to spend the rest of the evening there, Dave had to go. He was, he told me, off to attend a celebratory dinner, which was being put on for all of the British riders who had ridden the Tour de France.

My eyes lit up. I started imagining such a gathering

would take place in a wood-panelled dining hall in an exclusive gentlemen's club. There would be brandy, of course, cigars, too. And there would be a wonderful sense of achievement that drifted about the place like second-hand smoke. I doubted very much that this was the reality, but to me that dinner seemed like the consolidation of an idea I had of what it might be like to be a member of that exclusive British Tour riders' club.

A number of things made the idea of being a part of that elite group so special. There was, of course, the appeal that any club that doesn't want you is bound to have, but it was more than that. For as long as I could remember, I'd wanted to be, and to feel like, a professional bike rider. I had grown up believing that the way you could do that was firstly to race for a European professional team, and secondly to ride the Tour de France.

In a funny way, I had always figured that riding the Tour de France was what made you a *real* professional. The Tour is burned into the collective conscience of the British public as *the* bike race. The reasons why are multiple: the soap-opera-like appeal of the three-week narrative, the summertime slot, the reality that France is a stunningly beautiful country to look at, and, of course, the fact that for so many years Messrs Liggett and Sherwen made the Tour de France work so well as a televisual experience for an English-speaking audience.

And I wasn't the only one who thought so. There is one question that every person who has ever raced a bike for a living in the UK has, at some stage, had to answer with either a simple yes or a long-winded no.

Have you ridden the Tour de France?

It's the equivalent of asking someone who claims to be an actor if they've been on TV, or a musician whether they've been on *Top of the Pops*; it's a question that helps to define a less well-known profession to a wider audience. But these crude dividing lines inevitably get passed from the audience to the participant, and in time they become the standard by which the individuals judge themselves.

Cycling is a sport that's based on a staunchly traditional and historical calendar. A 'real' cyclist could tell you instantly why winning Ghent–Wevelgem is more important than winning the GP Waragem, but to the outside world they both look a lot like bike races. And that's where the Tour comes in: because of its fame it's almost the lowest common denominator. To riders, fans and public alike, it can seem that the moment you ride the Tour de France, and you can finally say yes to *that* question, is the moment that you become a genuine professional cyclist.

In 'A Domestique's Tale' – his excellent piece for volume two of *The Cycling Anthology* – Dan Lloyd neatly sums up his pride at being able to finally answer yes to that question when he returned from the 2010

Tour. But in the case of Roger Hammond, Lloyd's former teammate at both Cervélo and Garmin, that question elicits a different response.

'It did actually get to a point in my career when I used to just make up different jobs rather than say I was a professional cyclist,' admits Hammond. 'You would get two questions: "So, do you ride in the Tour?" "No." "Oh, right, okay. So, have you done the Olympics?" "No." "Right." And that would be the conversation stopper, and it would always be really awkward. Eventually I rode the Olympics, so I could at least say yes to one of them.'

In some ways, Hammond is a genuine rarity: he is one of very few British cyclists to have had a successful career on the road in Europe without ever having ridden the Tour.

Ever since Brian Robinson and Tom Simpson broke ground for British cyclists in Europe in the fifties and sixties – and until very recently, when British riders have become global players – there has always been a constant and steady stream of British cyclists who have managed to turn professional in Europe. But European bike racing was very much the school of hard knocks, and a majority of these riders (including me) didn't, for one reason or another, last more than a few years. Those with more longevity usually found their way to the Tour eventually, and became household names. But every so often riders would get on with a career as a European professional cyclist without ever reaching the Tour.

I wondered what the difference was, really, between those who had and those who had just missed out, and yet carried on to have successful careers anyway. Do they see the Tour as something they still felt they needed to have done to have really made it? Was it a question that haunted them? And if they weren't riding the Tour, then what were they doing for all those years in the peloton?

HAMMOND'S CHOICE

With podium places in both Paris–Roubaix and Ghent–Wevelgem, as well as a string of other top ten places in the northern Classics, Roger Hammond is perhaps Britain's best-ever bike rider never to have ridden the Tour de France. As a result, you could argue he is also the best British bike rider that the general public will know the least about.

Unlike most who simply never had the chance, Hammond's reasons for not having ridden the Tour de France in a career that spanned well over a decade seem to be down to choices that he made to *not* do so.

Hammond grew up in the UK in the eighties and, like all aspiring riders of his generation, moved to Europe to pursue his dream of becoming a professional cyclist. Only in Hammond's case his dream didn't involve the Tour de France at all; instead he coveted a race that even fewer people in the UK would have heard of: Paris–Roubaix.

'My oldest cycling memory is of watching Adri van der Poel in Paris–Roubaix, and thinking, "Wow! What an event!" Roubaix and the Classics were the first races that I saw – the Tour only came much later for me – and so I think that's what influenced the way I rode, and what motivated me later on in life.'

For most British riders, an amateur career and eventual pro contract in Europe only served to increase the desire to ride the Tour. The majority who turned pro did so by going through the (then excellent) French amateur system, and duly ended up in French pro teams. With his heart set on winning Paris–Roubaix, however, Hammond took a slightly different path, combining racing cyclo-cross (in which he won a junior world title) with studying for an engineering degree at Brunel University, before eventually starting out his professional road career in Belgium, where he would base himself for his entire career.

Belgium, much like Italy, is a country so steeped in its own cycling traditions that the Tour is a genuine afterthought, for fans and riders alike. What really matters in Belgium are the Belgian races, namely the spring Classics: Ghent-Wevelgem, the Tour of Flanders and Paris–Roubaix.

'Nobody talks about the Tour de France in Belgium; everything is geared towards the Classics,' explains Hammond. 'The build-up starts at Het Volk [now officially called Het Nieuwsblad] at the end of February, and, from then on, all the way up until the last Classics in April, people are just talking about them and writing about them.

'Everybody in Belgium knows all the intricacies of the Classics: how they run, who the favourites are,' Hammond continues. 'They're just into it, and if people are into it, then you get the feeling that you're doing something almost more worthwhile.'

Unlike today when the internet and low-cost airlines allow expatriated bike riders to have one foot in a foreign culture while keeping up to date with what's happening at home, in the late nineties, when Hammond turned pro, British riders were genuinely isolated in their European bases. Hammond's self-imposed exile in Belgium served to remove him from UK cycling circles, which in turn meant he was less and less affected by how he was regarded in his home country.

When he took third place at Paris–Roubaix in 2004, it marked the first time in the race's 108-year history that a British rider had achieved such a feat. The British cycling press was, naturally, delighted, but the mainstream media hardly touched the story. The reverse was true in Hammond's adopted home of Belgium.

'After my podium in Roubaix, I was on two chat shows on Belgian television, as well as their version of *A Question of Sport*, plus another TV show. So that was four shows in Belgium, compared to none in the UK.'

I wondered, genuinely, if this bothered Hammond, but his reaction seems to suggest otherwise.

'It's about your environment, isn't it? You're not affected by what isn't your environment, so it was hard for me to understand or appreciate how my rides went down in the UK, because I wasn't UK based. I'd only come back for the national championships and then be back off to Europe again.'

It's a very pragmatic response that I find to be typical of many successful bike riders. Often, when you talk to the people who are in a position to ride the races that most people can only daydream about, their view lacks any of the romance that fans might attach to them. There is a balancing act between aspiration and realism that every bike rider has to be able to get right if they are ever going to be any good. Dreams, as valuable as they are, have to be achievable, and sometimes this can come across as quite uncompromising. When he talks about the Tour de France, Hammond is no different.

'I always rode races to try to win, and, realistically, however far-fetched my ambition was – and I believe that all bike riders should have far-fetched ambitions

– when I thought about Grand Tours, I thought, "Why would I go there?" Because, even in my wildest dreams, even if the winds were in all the right directions and I had the best three weeks of my life, I was never going to win the Tour de France. Why would I put all that effort into preparing for it just to ride around? I couldn't really see the appeal of it at all. The races I did were either preparation for what I wanted to do, or they were the races that I thought that I could possibly win.'

If his environment and his ambitions in the Classics were the main reasons that Hammond never aimed to ride the Tour, the other key reasons seem to be in part physical, and in part down to the timing of his career.

A powerful rider on the flat who excelled on short, punchy climbs, Hammond wasn't ideally suited to the Grand Tours. He readily admits that he was at his best in races that required an element of skill, and that he worked hard to make sure that in the Classics he could make up for any possible lack of strength by finding advantages elsewhere. While he may not have liked the long hard climbs of the Alps and the Pyrenees anyway, the era that he rode in compounded those issues.

'The Tour de France was always the changing point in the season for me. I'll give you an example: in April 2004 I was on the podium in Roubaix, and in July

I was thinking about giving up bike racing. It was
just ridiculous: the change in speed was ridiculous. I
mean, okay, there is a bit there in terms of motivation,
but I think that we can see now there was a lot more
going on.'

It's a harsh reality for Hammond that his career
coincided with a widespread doping culture that he
didn't want any part of. It's something that comes up
again when I ask whether he thought he would have
benefitted physically from riding a three-week tour
earlier in his career. The common belief at the time
was that a rider who went into a Grand Tour came
out a lot stronger, but as ever the reality may not have
matched up with the story.

'I saw more natural athletes end their careers at
Grand Tours than I saw build from them. For the first
ten years of my career, the few guys that I would still
put my hand in the fire for to say they were natural . . .
Not many of them came out better bike riders for it.'

It's murky water, and Hammond makes the point
not to cast any further aspersions, but to explain why,
for the first part of his career at least, riding the Tour
had so little appeal.

Over the years, Hammond developed beyond just a
Classics rider into an experienced road captain, and as
such his chance to ride the Tour nearly came in 2007.
Hammond had enjoyed a strong Classics campaign
riding for the T-Mobile squad and, as it happened,

the Tour was starting in London, in Hammond's own backyard.

'In 2007, I was part of the selection procedure, and at the time I remember thinking I was in with a shot. Then I got to the Tour of Switzerland and they said, "We aren't going to take you; we're taking Cav instead." I just said, "Okay – go on then." I was a little disappointed, but I can see now, just by the way I reacted, that I wasn't as bothered by it as the others maybe were.'

I wonder how Hammond really views this missed opportunity, because surely if ever there was a chance to be recognised in your home country, this would be it. As a home rider taking part in the Tour, he would be on every TV and in every newspaper in the country, all the recognition one could ever desire. But the realist in Hammond puts me straight.

'As much as it excited me to start in the UK – it is always amazing to ride a major event at home – I do remember thinking that if I started then in three days I'd be back across the Channel, and then I had to do the other bloody two-and-a-half weeks of it!'

In truth, Hammond was getting all the plaudits he needed –the fame, the respect, the salary – he was just getting them elsewhere. What was more, he was getting them without having to ride the Tour, a race that simply didn't suit his talents as a rider, nor fulfil any personal ambition.

Despite that, does he not feel like he missed out in some way by never riding it? Such is the draw of the Tour that Hammond, like almost everyone I speak to who didn't ride it, still has a conflicting opinion on whether they regret never doing it.

'Every so often I think, "Perhaps I should have just concentrated on it for a year and ridden round" – just so I could answer yes when people ask if I've ridden it.'

But, just as quickly again, Hammond displays the balance between realism and ambition that he managed to master so well as a rider.

'It's just the rose-tinted glasses part of me that thinks you just have to turn up and ride round for three weeks and go home. The other part of me is the realistic person that knows what it takes, and knows how many sacrifices I would have made for it. Would I have sacrificed one chance of trying to win Roubaix for a ride at the Tour? No.'

LODGE'S LUCK

There's more than one type of professional cyclist. There are those who have the potential to win big, and there are those who may not ever get near a big win, but who still make themselves valued in the professional peloton.

It's obvious why riders in the first category can

usually find themselves a professional contract in a big European team. Not only do they often come with a sack-load of UCI points, but teams know that, if everything goes well, they have a potential winner in their ranks. And winning, after all, is a universal language.

Roger Hammond is a rider who clearly fitted into this first category. European teams knew that on his day he had the potential to win the biggest one-day Classic of them all: Paris–Roubaix. As such, his time in the professional peloton makes a lot of sense. Hammond may never have ridden the Tour, but there is no doubt that he was a big name in the sport.

But for riders in the second category, who may never have come close to the big win, life can be a lot tougher. There are simply more people who want to be professional cyclists than ever can be. There are no spots on a professional team that can be given away easily, and in the case of British riders, who until very recently were outcasts in the closeted world of European cycling, a ride was hard to come across and even harder to keep. The reality was that British riders were strangers in a foreign world and there was always a reason for signing a rider from the home nation of the team over a British rider.

More than likely, this is why there are countless numbers of British riders who turned professional only to return to the UK after just a couple of years, with their dreams of ever riding the world's biggest races gone for ever. They may have been good bike riders, but they weren't big winners, so they were replaced by a Frenchman or an Italian, riders who could do the same job, but whose faces fitted much better.

That's what makes the career of Harry Lodge so exceptional to me. Lodge was a professional cyclist for thirteen years, during which time the quietly spoken Wiltshire man rode the tours of Italy and Spain, as well as all of the world's greatest one-day Classics, and virtually every race on the professional calendar bar one: the Tour de France.

Lodge is a British rider who simply got on with the job of being a continental-based professional, and did so with practically no fanfare or profile in his home country. Lodge began his racing career in the UK in 1986, and soon realised that if he wanted to make a living out of riding his bike, he was going to have to leave the UK scene far behind.

'For starters, I wasn't a sprinter,' says Lodge, 'so I knew it wasn't going to happen with the racing being so focused on the criterium series in the UK, and outside of the crits there was just no program of racing, as far as I was concerned.'

Far from being outcast by the British cycling world, Lodge spent two years as an amateur, racing as part of the national-team set-up, which culminated in a place in the four-man team time-trial squad at the 1988 Seoul Olympic Games.

But he had his heart set on a professional career, and spent the 1989 season racing as an amateur in Belgium before signing for the small Belgian La William team. After a season there, he moved on up to the second-division Collstrop team.

'With Collstrop, I started riding big races,' Lodge explains. 'I was second in the GP de Cannes at the beginning of the year, then I was in the top ten of the Classic des Alpes, and I got up there in Liège–Bastogne–Liège. I was in the break all day there, and only got dropped on the last climb.

'So I was doing good races, and getting results in events like the GP de Wallonie and the Midi Libre. Because I was young, too, I started to get noticed by the bigger teams, and at the Wincanton Classic in August 1991, I signed with Tulip.'

When Lodge signed for Tulip Computers – the team of Brian Holm and Adri van der Poel, among others – it was a step into the big time. In 1992, the Belgian Tulip team was the equivalent of a UCI WorldTour team in 2014: the team had automatic entries into all of the world's best races, including the Tour de France.

Unlike Hammond, Lodge was well suited to stage races, and that was where his ambitions lay. At Tulip, he found himself a part of the stage-race squad, riding

Tirreno–Adriatico and Milan–San Remo before building up for his Grand Tour debut at the Giro. It was at
the Italian tour that Lodge's luck seemingly turned a
little, when a mistake by his mechanics cost him not
only a potential top-20 finish, but also his chance to
ride the Tour.

'I was down to ride the Tour, but I came out of
the Giro with a strained tendon, which came from
the mechanics putting long cranks on my bike at
the Giro without telling me,' Lodge explains. 'They
just assumed, because I was tall, that I rode 175mm
cranks, when in fact I rode 172.5.

'I didn't know anything about it to start with, but
after a while I started noticing that something wasn't
right, and by the last week I was having real problems.
After the Giro, I went back home to Salisbury and I
couldn't ride for ten days. I had to have ultrasound,
and I could barely ride my bike.'

He missed the Tour as a result, and, although
he recovered from his injury, Lodge's season ended
in more frustration when the Tulip team folded. It
would turn out to be Lodge's one and only chance to
ride the Tour, and he re-signed with Collstrop for the
1993 season.

'But at the end of 1993, a bit of an economic
slump hit northern Europe and there was something
like sixty riders out of contract. I found a place with
the Italian Amore e Vita team. Back then they had a

really good programme, including the Giro and the
Vuelta.'

Just as they do in Belgium, in Italy they have their
own opinion about which pro bike races are the most
important, and it tends to be their own calendar of
Italian races that counts, almost to the exclusion of
everything else, including the Tour de France.

'We rode the whole lot – all of the Italian Classics,
Tirreno–Adriatico, and then the Tour of Spain, too.'

The month of July, however – when the Tour de
France happens to take place – was very quiet. As anyone who has been to Italy in the summer months will
know, Italians take their holiday time as seriously as
they take mealtimes, and this can be as true for professional cyclists as anyone else.

As a journeyman pro, one of Lodge's key traits was
that he was able to fit in and do what was asked of
him. This went much further than being a good *domestique*, or learning Flemish and Italian; it also meant
that he would have to be motivated for the races that
his Italian paymasters wanted him to perform in. The
Italian cycling scene was so strong in the nineties that
there was usually very little need for Italian teams to
venture out of Italy. In practical terms, this meant that
a second-division team like Amore e Vita, which put
all of its resources into riding the Giro, had no chance
of – or interest in – riding the Tour de France. It also
meant that in the eyes of the British public – who

would have had little or no access to results from the smaller Italian races – Harry Lodge had, to all intents and purposes, disappeared.

It would be wrong to look at Lodge's exile in Italy as something that was forced upon him, though. He settled there, and married an Italian, and essentially just got on with it. In a country that adores cycling, where professional cyclists are genuinely revered, recognition in the pages of *Cycling Weekly* or the *Daily Telegraph* would have seemed completely pointless.

'Am I sad or despondent that people in the UK didn't recognise what I did as a rider? No – it's never bothered me, because my results were always recognised where I lived, in Italy and in Belgium.'

Even though he wasn't a rider of the stature of Hammond, as a professional cyclist in Europe, Lodge clearly got all of the recognition that he needed. Had he ridden for a French team, it's very easy to imagine that a rider with Lodge's qualities would certainly have ridden the Tour. But Lodge, like Hammond, views the Tour rather differently compared to most British fans of the sport.

'The culture in the UK is different. If someone's ridden the Tour, then that's brilliant. In Belgium, if you've ridden the Tour, it's a case of, "Okay, great, but what did you do?" If you were a workhorse, then, okay, they'd recognise that. But it is always, "What did you do?" The same question gets asked in Italy, and certainly in France, too. In the UK, and possibly in the States as well, the fact that you've even done the Tour, and perhaps finished it, is enough.

'Riding the Tour wouldn't have really made that much of a difference to me where I was living. It would have been nice to have ridden – I mean, it's every bike rider's dream to ride the Tour de France – but I wouldn't have wanted to go there just to tag along.'

It would have been much better for this piece if Lodge been bitterly disappointed that he missed out on the Tour, and if he'd blamed not riding it on a lack of recognition in the UK for his achievements. It might have made for a more heart-wrenching read. The truth is, Lodge looks back on his cycling career as it really was, and his attitude shows that he certainly doesn't dwell on the past.

'One of the things that you've got to always remember when you stop racing is that you'll be forgotten, and that the next generation will come along. Always. Whoever you are. There are people starting cycling in my club who haven't heard of Sean Kelly, and it will go on.

'For many riders, how much you'll be remembered is how much your hand will be missed when you pull it out of a bucket of water. And riders have to get that into their heads to make the transition into real life.'

Harry Lodge missed out on a ride in the Tour de France through a little bit of bad luck – an error of judgement on the part of a mechanic – but the fact is that to him being a professional cyclist in Europe wasn't just about that at all.

THWAITES'S WAIT

Whereas Hammond and Lodge raced in an era when British cyclists were very much second-class citizens, the recent successes of British riders at the highest level in Europe have seemingly awakened the world to their potential. As a result, the number of British riders in top professional teams has steadily risen, meaning that British riders are more likely to find their way to the Tour de France than ever.

Riders such as Peter Kennaugh and Ben Swift (who both rose through the GB Academy ranks to ride the Tour with Team Sky) serve as poster boys for the GB/Sky set-up, while others such as Steve Cummings (BMC), Adam and Simon Yates (Orica-GreenEdge) and Alex Dowsett (Movistar) will all be vying for spots in their respective teams' Tour squads.

But, outside of the WorldTour teams, there were three British pros for whom 2014 would possibly be their only chance to join the list of British Tour de France riders.

Scott Thwaites, Jonny McEvoy and Erick Rowsell ride for the German NetApp-Endura team – the result of the small, British-based Endura outfit merging

with the German NetApp squad at the end of the
2012 season.

In 2013, the team received wild-card invitations to
a number of WorldTour races, and a taste of things to
come when it was invited to ride the Tour of Spain,
organised by Tour de France parent company ASO.

In January 2014, ASO announced that the team
had managed to secure one of the four wild-card spots
on offer for pro-continental teams to ride the Tour de
France – a huge opportunity for the second-division
German outfit and its riders. While the Tour comes
around each year for the likes of Team Sky, there are
no guarantees at all for race starts for teams in the
pro-continental ranks.

For Thwaites, selection for the 2014 Tour, should
he get it, would come with the added incentive that
the *Grand Départ* would be in his home county of
Yorkshire. Riding the Tour de France on the very
roads you grew up on would be an amazing opportunity, but for Thwaites, a British professional cyclist in
a small European team, there is more to it than that.

In many ways, Thwaites and his companions currently fall through a gap: with Team Sky conquering
cycling on the world stage, and a strong resurgence
of UK-based teams racing week in and week out on
home soil, the British media have an abundance of
riches to write about. For Thwaites and his companions at NetApp-Endura, who race year-round in other

European professional events, appearing at the Tour has the potential to be the chance to get the attention they feel they deserve.

'The British scene has had a bit of a boom, so there's a lot of young British guys coming up, which has meant that the British press has tended to focus on them and Sky,' says Thwaites. 'We don't race in the UK much and, being on a German team – even though [Scottish brand] Endura is a part of it – the UK media sort of overlook us. But I think now that the Tour is on our calendar, they will obviously be following our progress a lot closer.'

Thwaites is only twenty-three, and, unlike Hammond or Lodge, isn't looking back at his career, he is looking forward. As such, his desire to ride the Tour isn't simply about raising his profile now, or indeed in the future, it is also about the practical and professional benefits that could come with a ride there.

'I think a three-week race like the Tour gives you that extra bit of strength, especially at my age. The longest race I've done so far is the Tour of Qinghai Lake in China, which was thirteen stages, and I felt the benefit of that. I've seen year on year that I've gotten stronger by riding longer and bigger races, and so I think the Tour would be a massive step to give me a brilliant base for the next few years.'

Realistically, too, the Tour would be a huge shop window for a rider like Thwaites. The Tour is a marketplace for cyclists and teams, and in cycling being in the right place at the right time creates a lot of opportunities.

'If you can ride well and get a result at the Tour, or even just show that you are strong, then that's where the teams are looking,' Thwaites points out. 'There are a lot of riders that can do well in the small races, the 1.1 and 1.2-ranked races, but the big WorldTour teams want riders who can compete on a WorldTour level, so that's really the stage on which you've got to show yourself.'

But for all that NetApp-Endura's inclusion in the race is amazing news for the three British riders in the team, for Thwaites and the others there's a harsh reality to riding for a twenty-one-man team that would only be able to send nine riders to the race. With the Tour presenting such a big opportunity to those that get to ride it, you can be sure that every single rider in the team wants to do just that.

Given his age and his talent, if 2014 wasn't to be his year, you'd think that another chance to ride the Tour could come for Thwaites. But in pro cycling, it's impossible to ever predict what might happen. Former British professional Jeremy Hunt – now Thwaites's coach – famously turned down the chance to ride the Tour as a young pro, believing that the chance would come around again soon enough. Hunt had to wait fifteen years for the opportunity again, during which time he had all but given up hope of ever riding it. He eventually rode it – and finished it – in 2010.

As a non-French team, NetApp-Endura won't be able to rely on getting a Tour wild card every year. While the opportunity to ride could put Thwaites in the frame for a contract with a bigger team and further opportunities to ride the Tour, not riding the Tour could also limit his options to staying with a team in the second division, where the chance to race the Tour doesn't come along that often, and the ago-nising wait for wild-card places that can hinder riders' preparation.

Much like Hammond, Thwaites is more suited to races other than the Tour. He is a fast-finishing rider who is at his best on tough, punchy courses, and he has other big races in his sights. He cites both Flanders and Roubaix as races he would love to target in the future. For now, though, in the eyes of the twenty-three-year-old who, having seen the Tour on TV as a child, 'went out and rode all the climbs in the Alps and was really inspired by that', there is no doubt that the Tour is the one.

'In thirty years' time, if I'm just riding to the café, then the people there will still remember that I'd rid-den the Tour. It would be a pretty big privilege to be able to say that you'd done the Tour; it would be a tick in your career. If you've ridden as a professional, then people give you a lot of respect, but riding the Tour, because it's the biggest race in the world, it's one extra thing that people would give you credit for.'

Whether Scott Thwaites will be able to add his name to the list of British Tour de France riders remains to be seen. Either way, I would bet that, in fifteen years' time, he'll be looking back on a great cycling career, with or without having ridden the Tour.

* * *

The world of professional cycling can be a sea of complications, fickle trade winds and unpredictable currents, where achieving anything takes a mixture of dedication, determination and a lot of luck, and getting to a race like the Tour de France quite often can come down to chance alone.

Ultimately, whether a rider needs to ride the Tour to feel they have achieved what they wanted is entirely down to them. In Lodge's case, a ride at the Tour would have been nice, but would have changed very little. In Hammond's case, a ride would have likely been an inconvenience following the efforts he put in during the Classics, and for Thwaites, the possibility of a ride will be motivation enough to put him in the best form of his life, and inspire him to better things.

Bike riders long for success and recognition, and the Tour de France seems to offer that. Even as awareness of cycling rises in the UK, I have no doubt that the public will continue to judge riders by whether they have ridden the world's biggest race.

But surely that inevitable 'Have you ridden the Tour de France?' question should also pose another: 'Can you have a successful career without doing the Tour de France?'

The answer to this, of course, is clearly yes.

Tom Southam is a former professional racing cyclist turned writer. His first book, *Domestique*, which he co-wrote with Charly Wegelius was released in June 2013. He is a regular contributor to *Rouleur* and *Soigneur* magazines. Born in Penzance in Cornwall, he currently resides in Bristol – the country's most liveable city. Most people will know him as the good-looking one in the Rapha adverts.